The Arno Press Cinema Program

THE MOTION PICTURE
IN THE SOVIET UNION: 1918-1952

A Sociological Analysis

By

John David Rimberg

ARNO PRESS
A NEW YORK TIMES COMPANY
New York • 1973

This volume was selected for the
Dissertations on Film Series
of the ARNO PRESS CINEMA PROGRAM
by Garth S. Jowett, Carleton University

First publication in book form, Arno Press, 1973

THE ARNO PRESS CINEMA PROGRAM
For complete listing of cinema titles see last pages

Manufactured in the United States of America

Publisher's Note: This volume was reprinted
from the best available copy.

- -

Library of Congress Cataloging in Publication Data

Rimberg, John David, 1929-
    The motion picture in the Soviet Union: 1918-1952.

    (The Arno Press cinema program. Dissertations on
film series)
    Originally presented as the author's thesis, Columbia,
1959.
    Bibliography: p.
    1. Moving-pictures--Russia. 2. Moving-pictures--
Social aspects. I. Title. II. Series: The Arno Press
cinema program. III. Series: Dissertations on film
series.
PN1993.5.R9R5 1972   301.16'1   72-559
ISBN 0-405-04100-4

THE MOTION PICTURE IN THE SOVIET UNION, 1918-1952:

A SOCICLOGICAL ANALYSIS

John David Rimberg

1959

Submitted in partial fulfillment of the requirements

for the degree of Doctor of Philosophy

in the Faculty of Political Science,

Columbia University

ABSTRACT

The Motion Picture in the Soviet Union, 1918-1952:

A Sociological Analysis

John David Rimberg

Students of the Soviet film industry have observed that the content
of Soviet films is determined by the art and propaganda policies of the
Communist Party. Some observers have also noted that film artists
employed in Soviet studios have influenced the content of films, although
artists are usually not members of the Communist Party. A few social
scientists have suggested that film audiences, too, have definite preferences regarding film content, and that these preferences are taken into
consideration by the Soviet film industry.

The thesis of this dissertation is that both film content and the
volume of film production in the Soviet Union are determined by a process
of compromise between Communist Party officials, film industry artists
and the Soviet audiences who constitute the primary potential market for
the exhibition of Soviet films. Compromise is necessary because the
Party prefers political content, the artists prefer to create works of
art and the audiences prefer entertaining films. Although these three
preferences are not mutually exclusive, the divergent views need to be
reconciled each time a film is produced. In the absence of successful
compromise, the Party may choose to ban the exhibition of a film or even
to interrupt its production, the artists may refuse to contribute their
services, and the audiences may refuse to attend when the film is

exhibited. Therefore the need for compromise is inescapable, if the Soviet film industry is to exist at all.

There is considerable evidence to substantiate this thesis. Sharp declines in the volume of film production can often be traced to a breakdown in the process of compromise. A comparison of the volume of film production and the extent of political propaganda content in films from year to year reveals an inverse relationship. The periods of maximum film production (1923-1928 and 1934-1945) coincided with the periods when propaganda content was relatively low. Vice versa, the periods of low film production (1929-1933 and 1946-1952) were characterized by increased political pressure for propaganda, resulting in a substantial decline in the number of film artists participating in productive activity at Soviet studios. In addition, an opinion survey among Soviet film-goers suggests that entertainment is the primary concern of the movie audience, which is prepared to accept only a limited amount of political propaganda. Therefore, the majority of films released by Soviet studios reflect compromises concerning film content to accommodate the conflicting views of the Communist Party, the film industry artists, and the potential film audiences in the USSR.

TABLE OF CONTENTS (Continued)

1

INTRODUCTION

"If political conditions comparable to those now existing continue in force and Soviet film producers are no longer periodically found guilty of creating ideologically deficient films, the necessary conclusion will be that the scenarists and directors have ceased to be artists and have become mere technicians."
—Alex Inkeles, Public Opinion in Soviet Russia, 1950

From the title-page of the book, to the final sentence of the chapter on films quoted above, the "pilot" study of Soviet mass communications media by a professional sociologist suggested numerous topics for future analyses of the Soviet film industry. Among these topics were public opinion, political conditions, film art and criticism. More concretely, attention was directed to motion-picture audiences, political leaders, and the "creative personnel" of the Soviet cinema studios.

The thesis proposed here interprets the history of the Soviet film production and content as the continuing accommodation of conflicting views on the purpose(s) of motion-pictures. All persons with the power to make decisions affecting Soviet film production and exhibition are parties to the conflict; many are also partners to subsequent agreements. On some occasions people with like opinions on the raison d'etre for films band together and act in concert. Specific social roles in Soviet society are conducive to one or another definition of cinema. These definitions are not always immediately compatible but are often subject to compromise. Accommodation of views within and between three powerful groupings—political leaders, artistic personnel, film audiences—is a

necessary (though not sufficient) condition for the survival of the
Soviet motion-picture industry as now constituted. Two other groups--
the administrators and the film critics--reflect the interaction between
differing opinions and the compromises which may result.

The thesis proposed here is based on at least three sources of inspiration. The first of these sources are the relevant theories and
data accumulated through the work of social scientists who have done
research on subject-matter broadly analogous to the topic of this study.
Second are previously published interpretations of the Soviet motion-
picture industry. The third source of inspiration are the data about
the Soviet film industry available to the writer as a result of his own
studies of primary and secondary materials, such as films, books, articles,
interview notes and other recorded information about motion-pictures in
the U.S.S.R. The present thesis is believed to be an advance over
earlier interpretations of the Soviet film industry and is in accord
with some currently accepted theories in related areas of scientific
research. The thesis put forward is held to be fruitful for analysis
of the considerable data on Soviet films presently available and may
also be useful for interpretation of fresh information as it becomes
available to social scientists in the future.

Several reservations ought to be noted. The adequacy of the hypothesis presented by the writer needs to be examined by other scholars in
possession of relevant data; the present work, consisting of thesis and
facts, is thereby justified. Research will be necessary in the future
to study additional data--those already accessible which may have been
inadvertently omitted, and those which will become available to social

scientists at a later time. Both of these review procedures will increase the value of the present work by refining the hypothesis. Another scientific contribution would be to link the theory presented here with other relevant generalizations so as to increase our understanding of the network of systems of which the Soviet film industry is an integral part. Several examples follow: The unique features of various territorial regions of the Soviet Union must be better understood and this could increase our knowledge about the particular characteristics of the film industry's branches located in various Soviet republics. Our understanding of Soviet writers in general can be improved by relating the film scenario-writers to novelists, dramatists connected with the theater, poets, librettists and so on. Studies of the U.S.S.R. Ministry of Culture and the Department for Propaganda and Agitation of the Communist Party could also generalize the thesis of the present work.

By way of acknowledgment, this essay owes its existence not only to those whose works are mentioned in the next chapter—but to many others, too numerous to mention. Nevertheless, the author wishes to express his gratitude to Dr. Alex Inkeles and Dr. Herbert Hyman. Dr. Inkeles not only kindled and encouraged the author's interest in the topic of this study, but also made accessible the relevant materials accumulated by the Russian Research Center of Harvard University operating under a contract with the U. S. Air Force, AF(33)-038-12909, the project on the Soviet Social System.[1] Dr. Hyman undertook to sponsor this present work, and patiently supervised it from inception to completion. To both scholars the author's indebtedness is gratefully acknowledged.

---

[1]Reproduction of this essay in general, and Chapters IV and VII in particular, is permitted for any purpose of the U. S. Government.

PART I

A REVIEW OF PREVIOUS RESEARCH STUDIES

CHAPTER I

STUDIES IN THE SOVIET FILM

A number of competent social scientists, film historians and critics
have written well-documented books and articles devoted to objective
description and analysis of the Soviet film industry prior to the end
of the Stalin regime (1953). In each of these studies, the respective
authors array substantial quantities of factual data into implicit analytic frameworks which vary somewhat from case to case but which also
have important elements in common. Although these writers are all well
acquainted with "the facts" (often as a result of direct participation
or observation), examination of the theoretic bases implied in these
studies has revealed their biased perspectives through the unresolved
problems in the various presentations, while suggesting a more comprehensive hypothesis to the present writer for understanding the Soviet
film industry.

All students agree that Soviet motion-pictures are social products
and that film content can best be explained in relation to the interaction
of several social groups in the Soviet Union. The three groups most frequently singled out are creative artists (especially film directors),
political authorities, and motion-picture audiences.

These studies were generally limited to an analysis of the relation
between pairs of these three social groups. Some students focused attention on the interplay between creative artists and political authorities;

others concentrated their analysis on the relation between political authorities and film audiences in the U.S.S.R. (Hardly anyone explored the interaction between audiences and creative artists.) None of these students of the Soviet film adequately considered the simultaneous inter-action between all three major social groups and their respective sub-groups.

The restricted focus found in earlier studies of the Soviet film industry was paralleled by another significant theoretical limitation. By considering only two (out of three) major social groups at a time, and by treating each major group as homogeneous, earlier students were inclined to see the relation between groups as an unequal struggle in which one major group, usually the political authorities, consistently had the upper hand. A few students went so far as to suggest that a "triumph" by the political authorities was not only possible, but close at hand. (Some writers also discarded objectivity to applaud or condemn the alleged domination of the film industry by political authorities.) By disregarding one major social group, minimizing the power of a second group, and exaggerating the influence of a third group, the students of the Soviet film consistently oversimplified actual power relationships and reached doubtful conclusions not entirely warranted by the facts.

Taking for granted the stability of the Soviet film industry as an institution, the earlier studies failed to consider the possibility that the subjugation of one or more key groups in the Soviet film industry would result in deterioration and even paralysis of Soviet film enter-prises as presently constituted. Some students claimed to recognize some signs of deterioration in the artistic quality of films, but the importance of marked declines in film production was sometimes disregarded, and the significance of repeated "box-office" failures was frequently overlooked. None of the earlier studies adequately evaluated these trends and symptoms of instability. The power of major social groups (e.g., artists and audiences) outside the formal hierarchies of influence was consistently underestimated, and students of the film industry also failed to perceive the active antagonisms between several competing bureaucracies within formal influence hierarchies, namely, the Communist Party, the secret police and the government film administration.

Published Interpretations of the Soviet Film

Huntly Carter

Several books by Huntly Carter, a British critic of theater and film, interpreted the Soviet cinema as a laboratory for artistic innovation and for new administrative forms of bureaucratic state patronage. Carter's first-hand observations and interviews in the U.S.S.R. during the 1920's led him to describe many facets of the film industry, especially in his book The New Spirit in the Cinema (1930). He noted the variety of "film theories" (e.g., proposed definitions of the cultural meaning of the motion-picture) sponsored by enthusiastic young movie directors in Moscow, Leningrad and Kiev. Carter also pointed out that administrative control of the film industry was being exercised primarily by some local and regional government organs, and that centralized control was more apparent than real. He noted that the film industry still lacked adequate facilities and funds. To illustrate the economic deficiencies, he detailed the physical condition of movie theaters in

Moscow, using such phrases as "worn-out projector," "ancient screen"
and "dust-hole . . . badly in need of repair" to depict typical exhibition facilities in the Soviet capital.[1] About the audiences Carter said
almost nothing. Nevertheless his books provided valuable insights and
data concerning artistic freedom and the limits of state control over
the Soviet film industry before 1930.

Samuel Harper

Civic Training in Soviet Russia (1929) was written by the American
political scientist Samuel Harper on the basis of his trip to the Soviet
Union around 1928. The population of the Soviet Union, according to
Harper, was a vast student body undergoing a long period of political
tutelage at the hands of the Communist Party. Film audiences in the
U.S.S.R. were pupils (often recalcitrant pupils) exposed to periodic
doses of Communist political propaganda on the screen. Harper glossed
over the decentralized character of political controls in the film industry (in 1928) and the great variety of artistic opinions noted by
Carter. That one Soviet film had been exhibited countless times to an
unlettered audience in a remote Siberian village as a result of a
bureaucratic error seemed significant to Harper. He also observed, however, that urban Soviet citizens, children included, preferred "escapist"
foreign films to Soviet pictures,[2] while spokesmen for the Communist

---

[1]Carter, H., New Theatre and Cinema of Soviet Russia, London, Chapman and Dodd, 1924, pp. 240-41.

[2]Harper, S., Civic Training in Soviet Russia, Chicago, University
of Chicago Press, 1929, p. 334.

Party demanded the elimination of politically neutral films from exhibition facilities (nominally) under State control.[3] Harper did not
study the influence of creative artists in the film industry, nor did
he consider the significance of controversies within the ranks of the
Communist Party. Rather, Harper's interpretation of the Soviet film
industry centered on the latent antagonisms between film audiences and
an allegedly monolithic Communist Party that exercised administrative
control over the motion-picture through the State bureaucratic apparatus.

Winifred Bryher

The British author of Film Problems of Soviet Russia (1929) visited
the Soviet Union during the 1920's and wrote under the pseudonym of
Winifred Bryher. As in Carter's books, attention was focused on the
many artistic theories advanced by innovating Soviet film directors.
Entire chapters were devoted to the ideas and films of Eisenstein,
Pudovkin, Abram Room and the dean of the new State Film Institute, Professor Kuleshov. Two chapters on "the sociological film" illustrated
the myriad interpretations of Communist ideology expressed by numerous
Soviet film directors of lesser renown. Bryher also discussed the
directors in the Ukrainian film industry at Kiev, Odessa, Kharkov and
Yalta, but overlooked the significance of their leanings to "Ukrainian
nationalism." Bryher's interpretation of the "film problems of Soviet
Russia" ignored motion-picture audiences and administrative controls,
merely hinted at the financial difficulties confronting the film

---

[3]Ibid., p. 332.

industry, but yielded fresh ideas and abundant data on the complexities
of expressing a new political ideology in the motion-picture medium.

Joseph Freeman

As one of the three joint authors of Voices of October: Art and
Literature in Soviet Russia (1930), the American writer Joseph Freeman
contributed the chapter on "the Soviet cinema" in that book. His interpretation, based on a visit to the U.S.S.R., was partly concealed under
mountains of data, but comparisons with Carter, Harper and Bryher reveal
Freeman's greater sympathy for the viewpoint of the Communist Party in
the Soviet Union. He accepted the very optimistic statistics of the
first Five-Year-Plan as reasonable figures, and echoed accusations of
"formalism" voiced by Communist Party critics against "fellow-travelers."
Almost all indications of economic difficulties or administrative problems in the Soviet film industry were conspicuously absent from Freeman's
account. He did hint that Soviet film audiences preferred entertaining
films, but Freeman added that their desires would somehow be reconciled
with the regime's insistence on propaganda (which he euphemistically
labeled "accuracy," that is, truth);[4] no further details were given on
this very significant issue. Freeman's interpretation was not much
more than an uncritical acceptance of Communist claims, comparable to
any survey article on the Soviet film industry that might have been
written by a contributor to a Soviet encyclopedia under Communist auspices. Aside from the wealth of details on carefully selected topics,
Freeman's account was valuable chiefly for an image of the Soviet film

---

[4]Freeman, J., Voices of October, New York, Vanguard Press, 1930,
pp. 259-60.

industry very nearly synonymous with the idealized Communist point of view.

Aleksander Arosev

In honor of the fifteenth birthday of the Soviet film industry, an English-language book with the title Soviet Cinema (1935) was published in Moscow under the editorship of Aleksander Arosev, an "Old Bolshevik" Russian writer of novels and scenarios. It described many facets of the film industry in numerous optimistic essays by Soviet authors. This official history book of the Soviet film industry contained no hint of any problems confronting the Communist Party or the Soviet government in implementing their widely advertised plans for the film industry, save for a few veiled references to temporary technical difficulties of a minor nature. The book briefly noted that the highest Soviet award, the Order of Lenin, had been conferred on several persons in the film industry for the first time: the list of recipients did not include the internationally famous film director Eisenstein, but was headed by the government administrator controlling the industry, Boris Shumyatsky. There was not the slightest indication that Shumyatsky was shortly to be purged, together with his deputies, amidst official accusations that they had "deliberately disrupted plans, delayed the release of films, squandered the people's money, increased spoilage, and run up production costs."[5] Soviet Cinema came closer to

---

[5]"Delo chesti rabotnikov kino" (A Matter of Honor for Movie Workers), Izvestiya, March 26, 1938.

an empty boast than to a realistic picture of conditions in the film
industry. Nevertheless Arosev, the author, was executed for disloy-
alty in 1936.[6]

Richard Ford

A new interpretation of the Soviet film industry based on first-
hand observations by a British student of films was published during
1937, a year of purges and upheaval in the U.S.S.R.[7] Richard Ford's
brief article "Moscow Goes to the Movies" appeared in Sight and Sound,
a magazine published by the British Film Institute. Ford's study concluded that inefficiency and inadequacies characterized production and
exhibition at the lower levels of the governmental film administration.
In phrases reminiscent of Carter's observations a decade earlier, Ford
noted worn-out projection equipment, weak illumination, inferior film
stock, poor sound reproduction and careless operators. In marked contrast with the unconcern displayed by projectionists and other film
industry employees, Ford noted that motion-picture audiences were often
serious and tense: "The audience stares at the screen as if attending
an important lecture. Its attention seldom wanders. There is very
little laughter . . ."[8] Ford added, however, that some types of film
content, such as fast pursuits, love scenes and outright clowning put

[6]Babitsky, Paul, The Soviet Film Industry, New York, Frederick A.
Praeger, 1955, p. 158.

[7]Ford has also published Children in the Cinema (1939), the British
equivalent of W. W. Charters' Motion Pictures and Youth (1933).

[8]Ford, R., "Moscow Goes to the Movies," Sight and Sound, London,
1937, p. 11.

the audiences into gayer moods.[9] The interpretation suggested by Ford
stressed deficiencies in the bureaucratic management of facilities and
personnel in the Soviet film industry. He also considered significant
the generally serious attitude to films on the part of the Soviet audience.

Thorold Dickinson and Alan Lawson

A special supplement to the August issue of the British film industry
journal Cine-Technician was devoted to an eye-witness report by Thorold
Dickinson and Alan Lawson, both professional film producers employed in
the British motion picture industry. Dickinson and Lawson reported in
detail on Soviet film production as well as exhibition. They specified
the political restrictions that had been imposed on artists, including
limitations on art subject-matter and on foreign contacts.[10] Noting the
abundance of "dull" films with stereotyped roles, they concluded that
"avoidance of characterization in drama amounts to a steady weakening
of influence."[11] They evaluated the technical quality of film exhibition
and arrived at the same conclusions reached by Ford some months earlier,
without corroborating Ford's observations on Soviet film audiences.
Dickinson and Lawson, noting a decline in the quality of artistic films
and low standards of technical quality in production and exhibition, interpreted the Soviet film industry as an example of the deleterious

---

[9]Ibid.

[10]Dickinson, T., and A. Lawson, "The Film in USSR, 1937," Cine-
Technician, August 1937, pp. 109-10.

[11]Ibid., pp. 108-109.

consequences of excessive political control over film production and exhibition.

Kurt London

In his book <u>Seven Soviet Arts</u> (1938), the European art critic Kurt London[12] interpreted recent developments in the motion-picture industry as a split in the ranks of film directors brought about by the art policies of the regime. He concluded that "the leading film people in the [Soviet] Union have ceased to be avant-garde because they are afraid of being too venturesome. . . . Intense activity on the part of second-rate directors has recently eclipsed the work of the great men of the films. . . . The ukase of the new principles of art, and the doubtful interpretation of the concept of formalism . . . did more to cripple the standard of production than technical deficiencies of the studios and lack of artistic personnel."[13] As for film audiences, London noted that the views of the younger generation were often solicited at previews of children's films,[14] but he believed that audiences generally were the passive subjects of their regime: "The attitude of the masses both to the old and new art styles probably re-mains essentially dependent on the nature of the education afforded them."[15]

---

[12]London also published a book entitled <u>Film Music</u> in 1936.

[13]London, K., <u>Seven Soviet Arts</u>, New Haven, Yale University Press, 1938, pp. 293-94.

[14]<u>Ibid</u>., pp. 342-46.   [15]<u>Ibid</u>.

Dwight Macdonald

A number of articles about Soviet films were written by the American political writer Dwight Macdonald for publication in Partisan Review during 1938. Although scattered newspaper reports during 1936 and 1937 indicated that motion-picture production in the U.S.S.R. had fallen 80 per cent behind planned goals over a period of years, Macdonald was probably the first writer to state this significant fact with sufficient clarity. He concurred in the view that recent Soviet films had suffered "esthetic deterioration," becoming "banal and provincial." Macdonald, too, attributed this decline to recent changes in Communist art policies: "Not the fact of political control," he wrote, "but the direction of this control has been damaging."[16] Specifically, he cited such "Stalinist" art policies as the "campaign to convince . . . [the people] that they have already achieved the highest in the realm of culture,"[17] the campaign to isolate the Soviet Union from the West, and the campaign to inflate the images of political leaders.[18] Macdonald stressed that Communist art policy had encouraged both "classical" and "avant-garde" artists during the 1920's, with internationally famous results in both genres of film art. He also emphasized that social messages and propaganda had once been a source of inspiration to the most talented film directors, "but since 1930 the less politics in a film, the better it is likely to be."[19] Macdonald's interpretation of the Soviet film

---

[16]Macdonald, D., "Soviet Society and Its Cinema," Partisan Review, Winter 1939, pp. 80-81.

[17]Ibid., pp. 90-95.   [18]Ibid., p. 89.

[19]Ibid., pp. 80-81.

industry stressed the significance of quantitative (as well as qualitative) shortcomings in current Soviet motion-picture production. He
traced these deficiencies to official impositions on artistic freedom
during the "Stalinist" era, but he failed to relate them also to the
power of creative artists to protest objectionable government art policies. Macdonald criticized the "justification" that political curbs on
films were necessary to the "backward" Russian masses who could appreciate only "simple" art; he suggested instead that bans on artistic
freedom merely reflected Stalin's definition of "culture"—art that
could be easily manipulated by the Communist leaders for political ends.

Herbert Marshall and Jay Leyda

Two men with a strong admiration for the achievements of the Soviet
film industry spent several years in the U.S.S.R. before the second
World War to learn the art of film production from the internationally
famous Soviet director, Eisenstein. Herbert P. J. Marshall, a British
citizen and author of several articles on the Soviet film industry for
British periodicals during the 1930's, later published a booklet, Soviet
Cinema (1945), under the auspices of the pro-Soviet Russia Today Society
in London. Like Joseph Freeman, Marshall wrote with great sympathy for
the viewpoint of the Communist Party in the Soviet Union and omitted
discussion of most administrative difficulties confronting artists,
audiences and political leaders in their efforts to influence the content of motion-pictures. Although his interpretation undoubtedly idealized actual conditions in the approved Communist style, Marshall contributed useful data about the Soviet film industry's development before
and during the war years.

The other Eisenstein pupil, the American citizen Jay Leyda, translated his mentor's writings into English but published only three original articles himself, in Hollywood Quarterly and its successor Film
Quarterly. The first of these articles, on training of film workers in
the Soviet Union, seems to have idealized the subject somewhat, but on
the whole it was a valuable factual account. More scholarly and objective was Leyda's second article, a descriptive history of the Russian
film industry up to 1910. His third article, which appeared in 1959,
discussed the production of Eisenstein's last film, "Ivan the Terrible."
In 1959, it was reported (again) that Leyda was working on a "monumental
history of the Russian film."[20]

Nikolai Lebedev

Professor Nikolai A. Lebedev, a Soviet film historian (and film
director), wrote two books on the history of the Soviet motion-picture
industry (in Russian) that were published in Moscow. Lenin Stalin
partiya o kino (Lenin, Stalin and the Party on the Movie), which appeared in 1938, documented Communist political interest in films as
"agitation" (propaganda). Many statements by Lenin, Stalin and other
party leaders were quoted and party resolutions about the film industry
were reproduced, with a running commentary by Lebedev that stressed the
uniformity of Communist aims. In 1947 a longer and more detailed study
by Lebedev was published under the title Ccherk istorii kino SSSR.
I: Nemoye kino. (Outline History of the Movie in the USSR, Volume I:
The Silent Film). This work delved into the origins of the Russian

_____

[20]Film Quarterly, Berkeley, University of California Press, Volume
XII, Number 3, Spring 1959, p. 65.

film industry during the reign of the last tsar, Nicholas II, and
traced its development under the Soviet regime prior to 1930 (when sound-
films first appeared in Moscow). Lebedev's interpretation, which was
very carefully documented, depicted the evolution of Communist Party
control over the film industry as an extremely slow process punctuated
by frequent reverses. Resistance to the aims of Communist leaders was
frequently encountered during the 1920's, as audiences and artists
balked again and again. Difficulties with administrators and union officials were also noted by Lebedev. He credited the pre-1917 film industry in Russia with contributing artistic talent to the Communist-
sponsored studios in later years, and he also suggested that artistic
and technical innovations in western Europe and the United States had
inspired Soviet film artists. Lebedev was denounced by the Soviet press
in February 1949 for his "anti-patriotic bourgeois cosmopolitanism."[21]

Catherine de la Roche

Another history of the Soviet film was published by two British
citizens in London during 1948. Soviet Cinema was jointly written by
Thorold Dickinson, who described the era of silent films, and Catherine
de la Roche, who covered the sound-film period. Dickinson's views, when
compared with his previously published interpretation (reviewed above),
emerged substantially unchanged. Catherine de la Roche, who was a bit
more sympathetic to the Soviet regime, uncritically accepted the purpose
of films in the U.S.S.R. as this was generally defined by the Communist

---

[21]Izvestiya, February 27, 1949, p. 3.

Party: to lead the masses to Communism. Conceding that "naive . . .
clumsy . . . dull" films were produced in Soviet studios, she attributed these exclusively to "an insufficiency of talented or qualified
film makers, not policy."[22] Attempts to produce more "entertaining"
films after the second World War were explained by Catherine de la
Roche as follows: The root of the trouble [sic] was war weariness."[23]
She interpreted agreement with Communist aims as a necessary (but not
sufficient) condition for the flowering of artistic talent in the
U.S.S.R., and she viewed contrary aims merely as "trouble."

Alex Inkeles

The professional American sociologist Alex Inkeles turned his
attention to the Soviet film industry after he had completed his
pioneering sociological analyses of oral agitation, the press, and
radio in the Soviet Union. All four studies were subsequently published under the title Public Opinion in Soviet Russia (1950). (The
sub-title A Study in Mass Persuasion was far more descriptive of the
data and analyses to be found in his book.) His study of the film industry occupied only 25 pages in a book of over 250 pages, but it was
succinct and factually accurate.

An important lead to further study and analysis of Soviet motion-
pictures was contained in the second chapter of Inkeles' work, where

---

[22]de la Roche, C. (and T. Dickinson), Soviet Cinema, London, Falcon Press, 1948, p. 61.

[23]Ibid., p. 74.

Lenin's theory of public opinion was analyzed. "In the U.S.S.R.,"
Inkeles stated, "cost [of mass communication] is largely figured in
terms of the contribution the media are able to make to effective party
leadership. In that sense the propaganda and agitation carried by the
Soviet media are the functional equivalent of advertising in the United
States; both pay the way for the operation as a whole."[24] Advertising
costs in the United States are passed on to the consumers—at least
those consumers who buy advertised products—in such a way that consumers are generally oblivious to their full role in financing adver-
tisements, radio, and the press. Films, unlike the radio and press,
are not supported to a significant extent by advertising in the United
States or elsewhere. The cost of films is borne directly by the audiences most of the time and they are fully aware of this situation. Insofar as film production, distribution and exhibition costs are paid
directly and consciously by audiences in the Soviet Union, the audience
cannot be omitted from any complete study of the Soviet film industry.
For reasons beyond his control, Dr. Inkeles was forced to limit his
discussion of Soviet film audiences to less than two printed pages.
Nevertheless he concluded his description of the size of film audiences
in the U.S.S.R. with these words: "Audience resistance . . . must sig-
nificantly affect the impact of the film as an instrument for mobilizing
public opinion."[25]

---

[24]Inkeles, A., Public Opinion in Soviet Russia, Cambridge, Harvard
University Press, 1950, p. 24.

[25]Ibid., p. 307.

At least two other leads for further study were suggested by
Inkeles: changes in the "party line" on art, and the artists' powers
to resist ideological coercion. Dr. Inkeles stated at the outset that
the Communists intended to gain control over the film industry's administrative machinery and aimed for "complete ideological and artistic
subordination of the film to the needs and interests of the party,"[26]
but he also referred to many setbacks (in 1919, 1921, 1928, 1932, 1946)
sustained by the Communists as a result of changes in their art policies.
He also suggested the difficulties which "party line" changes posed for
administrators, including the "scapegoat" fate which ended some official
careers both in the party and government. (Nevertheless Inkeles made
no reference to the 1937 purge of the film industry's chief administrator Boris Shumyatsky and his deputies.) To seize possession of administrative offices was a relatively simple matter; to gain permanent and
unwavering control over all administrative officials was a more complex
problem for Communist leaders, as Inkeles implied.

Inkeles noted the vigorous resistance to Communist dictation which
was to be found among the creative personnel of the film industry. During the 1920's "many of the new films being produced in the Soviet Union
were made by people who were far from being strong supporters of the new
regime. As a result, the Soviet screen was filled with material considered antagonistic to the regime . . ."[27] Around 1930 the Communist-
sponsored Association of Revolutionary Cinema Workers "succeeded in
silencing many of the best talents . . . The effect of [this] period

[26]Ibid., p. 269.   [27]Ibid., p. 291.

on film quality was deleterious, to say the least, and this is acknowledged by Soviet authorities."[28] (Inkeles did not say, however, that
some talented artists "silenced" themselves deliberately to protest
Communist art policies.) During and after the second World War "many
Soviet producers" were making films considered frivolous and without
ideas,[29] and "major films [were] regularly produced which [were] found
politically and artistically unacceptable" to Communist leaders.[30]

After stating that the party's "goal is the complete ideological and
artistic subordination of the film to the needs and interests of the
party," Inkeles may have minimized the effectiveness of resistance by
artists when he predicted that "the outcome . . . is by no means in
doubt, but there are still at this late date sporadic flare-ups and
minor skirmishes which indicate that the battle has not yet been fought
to a completely successful conclusion for the Bolsheviks."[31]

Marie Seton

A 500-page biography entitled Sergei M. Eisenstein was published
in 1952 by Marie Seton, a British citizen who spent several years in
the U.S.S.R. during the 1930's and knew Eisenstein quite well. The
book was filled with new insights and facts about the interaction between creative artists, Soviet government officials and Communist Party
leaders. She recorded the many details of such interaction in this case-
study of the famous Soviet film director's life (terminated by a heart
attack in 1948), and interpreted his turbulent career as the expression

---

[28]Ibid., p. 294. [29]Ibid., p. 311.

[30]Ibid., p. 312. [31]Ibid., p. 289.

of a vital duality harboring both individualistic and conformist tendencies.

Seton noted "the contrast between Eisenstein's revolutionary views
on art and those of Lunacharsky, the Commissar of Education [during the
1920's], with all art projects in the Soviet Union under his control."[32]
She also pointed out Eisenstein's refusal to accept the definition of
films held by Boris Shumyatsky, the chief of the film industry from
1930 to 1937. After outlining the plot of a comic film-scenario,
"M.M.M.," Seton commented: "That Eisenstein should have proposed this
comedy to Shumyatsky showed how naive . . . [Eisenstein] was in his
estimate of official policy towards the development of comedy."[33]

Seton quoted Eisenstein's significant remark (made in a speech to
a conference convened to celebrate the fifteenth anniversary of Soviet
films, in 1935) that "the majority of the [artistic] people . . . came
to cinematography after having served in the Civil War in a technical,
not a leading capacity. We were like 'fellow travelers' in literature."[34]
Seton then paraphrased his subsequent remarks as follows: "But as the
country developed politically . . . the 'sideline' approach had been
broken up. More politically conscious people had entered the film industry . . ."[35] Eisenstein concluded: "My art is dedicated to no particular tendency but to the analysis of certain phenomena and ways of
thinking."[36] Seton recorded how Eisenstein's colleagues, including
film directors such as Sergei Vasiliev, Leonid Trauberg, Dovzhenko,

---

[32]Seton, Marie, Sergei M. Eisenstein, New York, A. A. Wyn, 1952,
p. 123.

[33]Ibid., p. 313.   [34]Ibid., p. 333.
[35]Ibid.   [36]Ibid., p. 336.

Yutkevich and Pudovkin attacked him so severely at the conference that
the director Kuleshov openly accused them of envy, and Nikolai Lebedev
pleaded that Eisenstein be allowed more time and facilities to develop
his art theories and work.[37] Eisenstein himself replied to his fellow
artists: ". . . only a talentless collective can exist in the face of
suppression of one creative individual by another. . . ."[38] He ended
his speech to the conference by praising the representative of the Communist Party's Central Committee, Sergei Dinamov, and the head of the
Soviet government's Chief Administration of Cinematography, Boris
Shumyatsky.

Shumyatsky halted the production of Eisenstein's next motion-
picture, "Bezhin Meadow," in March 1937, accusing the film director of
"harmful formalistic exercises." During a special conference convened
to discuss Eisenstein's failings, "not a single person came to the defense of Sergei Eisenstein," according to Seton, "nor did anyone suggest
that Shumyatsky's decisions be reconsidered."[39] After Shumyatsky was
purged in January 1938, a biographical pamphlet about Eisenstein explained that his "enemies" had suggested incorrect ideas, "confused his
goals, and offered useless materials," after which "the Party and the
Government, and Stalin in particular, came to his aid."[40] Seton may
have accepted this analysis at face value; in any case she did not offer
alternative interpretations.

---

[37]Ibid., pp. 339-40.

[38]Ibid., p. 349.

[39]Ibid., p. 369.

[40]Ibid., p. 379-87.

In 1946 Eisenstein suffered a very severe heart attack. For several months official criticism of his latest film ("Ivan the Terrible,"
Part II) was kept from him and from the public. "Eisenstein remained
in high esteem," according to Seton.

> The highest circles of the film industry and the Government at
> last recognized that no matter how eager . . . [Eisenstein] was
> to create a film in . . . [accordance with the Party] line . . .,
> once he commenced work he became so deeply immersed in his own
> complex ideas that he was carried away into regions remote from
> the public [sic]. Hence it was tacitly understood that for the
> remainder of his life he should be regarded as sort of "elder
> statesman," and, at the age of forty-eight, left to continue with
> his theoretical work.[41]

A few months later Part II of "Ivan the Terrible" was openly criticized
by the Central Committee of the Communist Party, and Eisenstein "wrote
a letter to Stalin. . . . In response to this letter, Stalin invited
Eisenstein . . . to visit him at the Kremlin. Stalin was apparently
sympathetic . . . and it was arranged that when Eisenstein was well
enough he should resume work. . . ."[42]

Marie Seton interpreted the Soviet film industry as the product of
inter-personal relations between artists and officials, as policy and
protest, as disagreement and compromise. In a brief article published
in 1954, entitled "Second Thoughts on Eisenstein," she wrote: "That
[Eisenstein] was hampered by current Soviet aesthetics cannot be denied;
but in the history of art what great innovator has not been hampered
by the aesthetics of his day? So long as there is periodic protest,—
the Soviet aesthetic will [continue to] develop."[43]   In 1952, Seton

---

[41]Ibid., p. 457.   [42]Ibid., p. 463.

[43]Seton, M., "Second Thoughts on Eisenstein," Soviet Studies, Volume 4, Number 2, pp. 122-23.

interpreted the criterion for production of any film in the Soviet Union
to be "the importance of its theme at a given time and the manner in
which it portrayed social and political reality."[44] In 1954 she added
the following reservation: "The inner nature of the artist varies enor-
mously as a result of his past life, his experience, and his character,
and, therefore, all artists cannot necessarily become 'infected' by the
same topically popular or important subject. When they [the artists]
attempt to comply without a true 'infection' with the subject, arti-
ficiality results."[45] About film audiences Seton wrote almost nothing,
but she interpreted the view of the Soviet government in what may be a
masterpiece of understatement: "The commercial value [of a Soviet film]
was of minor consideration; if it made money for the film trust which
produced it, so much the better."[46]

Paul Babitsky and Martin Lutich

Two separate essays on the motion-picture in the U.S.S.R. were published under one cover during 1954 in New York as The Soviet Movie Industry: Two Studies by Paul Babitsky and Martin Lutich. The essays
were published in Russian. Both authors were former Soviet citizens
who had been employed in the Soviet film industry as scenario-writers
during the 1930's; both left the U.S.S.R. during the second World War
and came to the United States.

---

[44]Seton, Eisenstein, 1952, p. 137.

[45]Seton, "Second Thoughts on Eisenstein," 1954, p. 119.

[46]Seton, Eisenstein, 1952, p. 137.

Neither Babitsky nor Lutich professed sympathy for the Communist Party's efforts to use films for political ends. Both clearly resented the Soviet bureaucrats, so ignorant of art; the "careerists" whose chief talent was their possession of membership cards in the Communist Party; the "informers"; and the ever-present police officials who made creative work, and sometimes life itself, difficult for the artists of the film industry.

Babitsky and Lutich interpreted the history of Soviet films as a reflection of "struggle"—the constant conflict between the Communist regime on the one side, film artists and audiences on the other. They rejected a Marxist or Hegelian interpretation of "struggle," however, for they saw no useful purpose nor ultimate synthesis in the conflict. Accounting for attendance at movie theaters in the Soviet Union, Lutich listed reasons such as these: 1) movie theaters were one of the few places where people could keep warm in winter; 2) daily life was so dull that Soviet citizens enjoyed films as narcotic dreams; 3) the artistry of actors, composers, and film-directors was widely appreciated; 4) audiences craved glimpses of life abroad, which explained also why any foreign film always drew the biggest crowds.

Babitsky cited numerous examples to support his view that many artists in the film industry had resisted political dictation by avoiding contemporary themes, by creating works with hidden meanings, by carrying Communist ideas to absurd extremes, by turning to other work (research, translation, instruction and so on), by subtle criticism and even by open protest. Both Babitsky and Lutich contended that Communist leaders sometimes contradicted one another in formulating and

interpreting official art policies, which added to the general confusion
and also provided film artists with additional weapons with which to com-
bat the political leadership. They also noted that the film industry
was sometimes in serious financial straits which incurred the displeasure
of party leaders, that audiences ignored Communist agitators' speeches
when these accompanied film showings, and that cumbersome censorship
procedures frequently crippled both the quantity and quality of Soviet
film production.

Babitsky and Lutich stressed the conflicts raging in the film industry, but they also noted that compromises did occur. Babitsky cited
occasions when film critics and censors "looked the other way" as Soviet
films low in political propaganda were released for exhibition. He also
noted that artistic personnel sometimes compromised their principles to
remain in the good graces of the Communist regime. Lutich suggested
that segments of the "older generation" of film audiences in the Soviet
Union had become "resigned" to Soviet films because foreign films were
less frequently exhibited as time went on. For both Babitsky and Lutich,
however, compromise was the minor theme and conflict was the key to interpretation of the Soviet film industry.[47]

Summary

Social scientists, film historians and critics in several countries
have followed developments in the Soviet motion-picture industry for
more than twenty-five years. Although interpretations varied considerably, all students attempted to be objective and apparently agreed that

_____

[47]Babitsky's views became available in English translation with the
publication of his book The Soviet Film Industry, New York, Frederick
A. Praeger, 1955.

the Soviet film could best be understood in terms of the interaction between several social groups. Nevertheless, none of the published studies attempted an interpretation based on all three key groups— political authorities, creative artists and film audiences. Instead, the writers limited their analyses to one or two of the three key groups. Freeman (1930), Arosev (1935) and Marshall (1945) concentrated on the political authorities—their aims, methods and achievements. Bryher (1929) focused on creative artists of the film industry. Harper (1929), Ford (1937) and Lutich (1953) analyzed the interaction between political authorities and film audiences. Carter (1930), Lawson (1937), Dickinson (1937, 1948), London (1938), Macdonald (1938), Lebedev (1938, 1947), Leyda (1946), de la Roche (1948), Inkeles (1950), Seton (1952), and Babitsky (1953) limited their interpretations to the relation between political authorities and the creative artists of the motion-picture industry. Virtually nothing was written about the simultaneous interaction between all three groups.

Another serious limitation resulted from the restricted focus just summarized. None of the studies adequately considered the delicate balance between these three key groups. The conflicts between them were not analyzed in terms of instability on the one hand, and compromise on the other. Stability was often taken for granted, and compromise was frequently overlooked. Consequently the essential dynamics of the Soviet film industry were neither fully described nor comprehended.

Nevertheless, without the wealth of data and important insights which these studies contributed, the present analysis would not have been possible. If this dissertation is an advance in understanding the Soviet film industry, this step forward is clearly based on previous work by those whose work has been reviewed.

PART II

DEFINITIONS: THE FUNCTIONS OF THE SOVIET FILM

CHAPTER II

POLITICAL DEFINITIONS OF THE FILM

". . . When the film belongs to the masses and is in the hands of
the real promoters of socialist culture, it will become one of the most
powerful media of mass enlightenment."
                                                        --Lenin, 1907

Karl Marx died in 1883 and Friedrich Engels died in 1895. Neither

lived to see the first public exhibition of a film in Paris on Decem-

ber 28, 1895. Although motion-pictures were exhibited in Petersburg,

Moscow, Nizhni-Novgorod, Rostov, Kiev and Kharkov in 1896 and were

thereafter regularly distributed in Russia by the French film companies,

Lumiere, Pathe and Gaumont, no films were actually produced in Russia

until 1907.[1] That same year, 1907, Vladimir Ilyich Ulyanov (who assumed

the name Lenin to disguise his identity) was hiding in Finland in a

small cottage together with Vladimir Bonch-Bruyevich (later the Execu-

tive Office of the Council of People's Commissars), A. Bogdanov, and

several other revolutionaries. Lenin had seen some motion-pictures by

this time, outside Russia. His first recorded pronouncement about the

functions of motion-pictures occurred when Bogdanov, who had just re-

turned from Petersburg, began to discuss films one day. According to

Bonch-Bruyevich, who was present at this discussion, Lenin said that

films "in the hands of crass speculators did more harm than good, as the

disgusting content of these films frequently corrupted the masses.

---

[1]Lebedev, Ocherk istorii, 1947, p. 13.

But," Lenin added, "when the film belongs to the masses and is in the
hands of the real promoters of socialist culture, it will become one
of the most powerful media of mass enlightenment."[2]

The Primacy of the Propaganda Function

Lenin viewed control of film content like any doctrinaire Marxist:
the ownership of the means of production would decide film content and
the cultural meaning of films. According to Lenin, audiences would see
any kind of film—good, bad or indifferent—and by implication the creative artists would contribute their skills to any production. Consequently the only real determinant of film content, in Lenin's opinion,
was the ownership of the production studios, distribution agencies and
exhibition facilities.

Lenin visualized two alternative meanings of films—one bad, the
other good—depending on the owner of the material facilities. In a
capitalistic economy the film was being used by the private entrepreneur
to enrich himself by exploiting the masses, according to Lenin; the
transfer of coins from the audiences to the exhibitors, distributors
and producers of films constituted the main purpose of the film in all
capitalistic systems, in Lenin's view. In a socialistic system, on the
other hand, Lenin thought that the profit-making aspects of the film
industry would lose significance, as the potentialities of the film as
a propaganda medium became paramount. When the masses become the owners
of production, distribution and exhibition facilities, Lenin observed,

---

[2]Lebedev, Lenin, Stalin, partiya o kino, 1938, pp. 7-8.

nobody would be motivated to exploit the masses financially by means of films; but some people would step forward to assume leadership in the film industry—on behalf of the masses—and would administer this industry chiefly for the purpose of producing, distributing and exhibiting films with content designed to "enlighten the masses."

As Lenin was of the opinion that the masses would be willing to see any kind of film at all, he did not anticipate any serious difficulties in getting people to attend the exhibition of "enlightening" films. Similarly, Lenin believed that creative artists would produce films to order—whether the orders came from a capitalist or a socialist—and Lenin did not expect any difficulties in obtaining the services of creative artists to produce films for "enlightenment."

When the Bolsheviks seized power late in 1917, the man who came forward to supervise the film industry in Russia was Anatoli Lunacharski, the first People's Commissar of Education of the Russian Soviet Federated Socialist Republic. Although the physical assets of the film industry were not specifically nationalized until 1919, Lunacharski's attitude from the outset was based on Lenin's definition of the role of films in a socialist state. Lunacharski concentrated his attention immediately on the propaganda potential of the film. By January 1918 a subdivision of the Commissariat of Education had been assigned the task of supervising the "educational" aspects of the film industry. Lenin's own wife, Nadezhda Konstantinovna Krupskaya, was appointed chief of this subdivision. At her direction, films were exhibited in the working-class districts of Petersburg free of charge, in line with Lenin's view that profit-making was superfluous in a socialist state. Most of the

pre-revolutionary films seized by the Bolsheviks were not well suited
to their propaganda needs, however, and production of new pictures was
hampered by meager supplies of raw film stock. Nevertheless, Lenin's
wife selected a few pre-revolutionary films from a collection owned by
a private social organization in Petersburg called the People's Library
Committee. Rejecting all films containing pro-Tsarist patriotic themes
or frivolous stories in a contemporary setting, she picked out some
filmed versions of nineteenth century Russian literary classics. As these
film plots contributed only a few themes useful to the Communist cause
(the evils of poverty, for example, or the problem of social injustice),
speakers were sent to "agitate" the film audiences with Bolshevik
harangues. In this context the films were used primarily as bait to draw
a crowd of working people so that they could be addressed by a speaker
armed with Bolshevik slogans and arguments.[3]

The entire film industry was nationalized in 1919, while civil war
raged in Russia. A decree signed by Lunacharski explained the purpose
of nationalization as follows: ". . . The transfer of the . . . movie
industry to the control of the People's Commissariat of Education [is]
for the accomplishment . . . of tasks in the field of scientific education, cultural development and agitation-propaganda . . ."[4]

-----

[3]Lebedev, Ocherk istorii, 1947, p. 66.

[4]"On the All-Russian Photo-Movie Department of the People's Commissariat of Education," Sobraniye uzakonenii i rasporyazhenii Raboche-
Krest'yanskovo pravitel'stva, 1919 (Collection of Enactments and Edicts
of the Workers' and Peasants' Government), Moscow, Yuridicheskoye
izdatel'stvo, No. 46, September 22, 1919, article 448, p. 491.

The emphasis on the propaganda function continued to predominate in the thinking of Communist leaders as time went by. In 1923, for example, Lunacharski wrote an article in the newspaper Rabochaya gazeta (The Workers' Newspaper) in which he quoted Lenin as saying that the film "is a powerful weapon of scientific knowledge and of the most effective agitation."[5] Writing in the same newspaper a few weeks later, the Communist leader Leo B. Rosenfeld (who assumed the name Kamenev) declared that "the film is a great medium for propaganda when it is in the hands of the proletariat."[6] In 1924, speaking at the 13th Congress of the Communist Party in Moscow, Joseph Djugashvili (who assumed the name Stalin) reminded the assembled Bolsheviks that "the film is the greatest medium for mass agitation."[7] In March 1928 a declaration was formulated at the nationwide Communist Party Conference on the Film: "The film can and must play a large role in the cultural revolution, as a medium of extensive education and Communist propaganda, [of] organization and education of the masses around the slogans and tasks of the Party, [of] popular art education, [and of] rest and entertainment when expedient." Note the qualification regarding entertainment! Professor Samuel Harper, who was in the Soviet Union that year, reported that "a speaker expressed the view that the film should serve exclusively as a means of relaxation. This opinion met with no support, however, and led to positive insistence that the motion-picture must be considered always as a means of education and training."[8]

---

[5]Rabochaya gazeta, May 22, 1923.   [6]Rabochaya gazeta, June 8, 1923.

[7]Lebedev, Lenin, Stalin, partiya o kino, 1938, p. 30.

[8]Harper, S., Civic Training in Soviet Russia, 1929, p. 333.

Two years later the famous motion-picture director Vsevolod Pudovkin, in an interview with a correspondent of The New York Times, commented that "the Soviet government is not interested in the cinema as a means of income. What is . . . more valuable . . . just now is educating our people."[9] The remark about the absence of the profit motive was especially significant because it was addressed to a representative of the American press; clearly, the comment was intended to suggest what Lenin had predicted many years earlier—that a socialist film industry differs from film companies in capitalist countries because it does not "exploit" the masses.

On the occasion of the "fifteenth anniversary" of the Soviet film industry in 1935, Stalin sent a message to Boris Shumyatski, who was at that time the chief administrator for all branches of the government-owned and government-operated film industry in the Soviet Union: ". . . in the hands of the Soviet regime, the film is a great, priceless force. Having exceptional opportunities to influence the masses emotionally, the film aids the working class and its Party to educate the working people in the spirit of socialism, to organize the masses in the struggle for socialism, and to raise their cultural and political fighting power . . ."[10]

Two weeks after Stalin's message was read to the film industry personnel gathered in Moscow, Mikhail Ivanovich Kalinin (who was Chairman of the Presidium of the Central Executive Committee, an office nominally equivalent to that of the President of the United States, or the Prime

[9] New York Times, December 21, 1930, Section 8, page 6.

[10] Lebedev, Lenin, Stalin, partiya o kino, 1938, p. 33.

Minister in Great Britain) spoke in Moscow's Bolshoi Theater in connection with the award of prizes to persons employed in the Soviet film industry. Speaking of the audience for Soviet films, Kalinin rephrased Stalin's comment about the effectiveness of films--in line with Lenin's views on this subject--saying that films "have the capacity to shape all the characteristics of man's personality." Then Kalinin stressed the universal appeal of motion-pictures, saying that "everybody loves the movies."[11]

Although Lenin's definition of the film's role in socialist society had not been limited to Russia, but to socialist states wherever they might emerge, more than 20 years elapsed before other socialist states came into existence. With their appearance the potential audience for Soviet films increased considerably, and the propaganda function now applied to a more numerous and still more diversified film audience. Motion-pictures were now to be produced with film content suited not only for audiences in the Soviet Union, but also for the North Koreans, East Germans, Albanians, Chinese mainlanders, Hungarians, and various other peoples living in socialist states.

As soon as the propaganda target of Soviet films was officially broadened to include audiences outside the U.S.S.R., the Soviet film industry was instructed by political leaders to challenge "Hollywood" all over the world. The personnel of the Soviet film industry were told in an Izvestiya editorial that they were "on the front lines of the ideological battle";[12] the newspaper Sovetskoye iskusstvo (Soviet

---

[11]Ibid., p. 78.   [12]Izvestiya, September 22, 1946.

Art) urged them "to enter into a merciless war with American motion-
picture expansion";[13] the magazine Iskusstvo kino (Film Art) proclaimed
the beginning of the "decisive battle with the self-righteous film art
of contemporary imperialistic capitalism."[14] Thus the Soviet film was
given a broader propaganda mission by Communist political authorities.

Still the basic political definition of the film had not changed.
Lenin's viewpoint was reflected again in a recent Pravda editorial that
labeled Soviet film industry personnel "engineers of human emotions"
and called on them to help the Communist Party in its efforts "to educate the people in the spirit of Communism."[15] Just before Stalin's
death, political authorities in the Soviet Union were still insisting
that the Soviet film must "propagandize the ideas of the Party of Lenin
and Stalin [and] the achievements of the Soviet socialist state."[16]

Other Functions

Despite their emphasis on the propaganda function, Communist
political leaders expected Soviet films to contribute other benefits
concurrently to the socialist state. While these other functions had
economic, educational, artistic and social aspects, they stemmed
principally from political considerations and were derived from the
evolving ideology developed by the Communist Party.

---

[13]Sovetskoye iskusstvo, November 23, 1957.

[14]Iskusstvo kino, Number 1, January 1948.

[15]Pravda, February 18, 1950, p. 3.

[16]Kultura i zhizn (Culture and Life), January 11, 1951, p. 3.

Soviet films were expected to compete with (and ultimately to displace) two traditional features of life in Russia: the church, and the tavern. The motion-picture was also expected to facilitate the dissemination of detailed scientific, technical and military knowledge--in particular by means of specialized films produced for this purpose. The film in the Soviet Union was considered to be an element of "culture" together with painting, music, the theater and so on; in this sense, the motion-picture was to provide popular relaxation and "culture," at the same time that it attracted creative artists to express themselves in this medium.

With the passage of time, still more political definitions of the film became evident. The motion-picture was exported from the U.S.S.R. to win sympathy and respect abroad for the achievements of the new socialist society, and also to earn foreign currency for the Soviet government in some of the more prosperous nations of the world. Nor was the income potential of domestic exhibition (i.e., film exhibition in the Soviet Union) ignored; some foreign pictures were imported by the U.S.S.R. so that the Soviet citizen would provide revenue to the Soviet State which owned virtually all domestic exhibition facilities.

The Film as Rival to the Church

A basic tenet of Communist ideology has been "materialism." Hostility to organized religion has always been fundamental to Communist doctrine, despite specific instances of compromise with church groups in the Soviet Union. The Communist-sponsored Society of Atheists actively opposed religious practices in any form; membership in the Communist Party was considered incompatible with membership in an organized church; Soviet leaders frequently denounced religion as "a remnant of capitalism in the mind of men." Nevertheless, Communist political leaders recognized that religion and the church were deeply rooted; they looked about for means of competing with the church.

Not long after the 1917 revolution, top-ranking political leaders perceived the motion-picture as one means of competing with the church for popular attention, interest and financial support. Lenin was quoted as having said that "art alone, and nothing else, can be a substitute for religion."[17] Trotsky wrote in Pravda that "meaningless ritual . . . cannot be destroyed by criticism alone; it can [only] be supplanted by new forms of life, new amusements, new and more cultured theaters. . . . The motion-picture amuses, educates, strikes the imagination through images, and liberates [people] from the need of entering the church door. . . ."[18]

Communist leaders continually looked to the film to rival the organized churches in the Soviet Union, and severely criticized any evidence of mysticism or religious feeling among film industry personnel— lest these sentiments be expressed in film content. Thus the famous film director Eisenstein was criticized, for example, for his interest in religion, and was denounced as a "God-seeker";[19] a decade later, he was again criticized in the official Soviet press for producing a film about "permanent and mystical forces of good and evil."[20]

---

[17]Kalinin, Mikhail Ivanovich, "Speech to the Fifth All-Union Congress of Art Workers," quoted in London, Kurt, Seven Soviet Arts, 1938, p. 19.

[18]Quoted in Evans, Ernestine, "The Soviet Idea in the 'Kino,'" Asia, August 1926, p. 700.

[19]Babitsky, Soviet Film Industry, 1955, p. 125.   [20]Ibid., p. 309.

The political leaders of the Soviet Union expected films to compete
with the church—not to lend support to any doctrine associated with
organized religion.

The Film as Rival to the Tavern

Vodka became the target of Communist criticism because vodka
was considered to have corrupted the morals of the citizenry, inter-
fered with orderly working habits, and drained off the wage-earner's
money income. The last of these objections was important especially
"under capitalist conditions," when the money derived from the vodka
trade benefited the private tavern owner, the distiller and the
"capitalist" government which taxed or monopolized the vodka business;
when the liquor industry was nationalized by the Soviet regime, the
financial aspect of the vodka trade was no longer considered an un-
mitigated evil by Communist politicians. Nevertheless, the other results attributed to vodka—immorality and inefficiency—continued to
confront Soviet leaders with a serious problem.

The motion-picture was soon perceived by Communist politicians
as a possible rival to the tavern. The income from films could
readily replace the income from vodka, these political leaders reasoned,
without the twin evils of immorality and inefficiency attributed to
the vodka trade.

Trotsky was one of the Communist leaders who saw the motion-picture
as a competitor to the "public house"—that is, the tavern.[21] Stalin,
too, spoke out in this vein. Addressing the fifteenth Party Congress

---

[21]Evans, loc. cit.

in December 1927, Stalin said in his Political Report (on behalf of
the Central Committee of the Communist Party): "I think that it shall
be possible to begin the elimination of vodka, by replacing it with
such sources of income as the radio and the film."[22] Subsequently,
political slogans issued periodically by the Communist Party included
this message: "Let the revenue from the motion-picture replace that
from vodka."[23]

The Film as Practical Instruction

In addition to its ideological teachings, Communist leaders expected Soviet films to give practical instruction in a great variety
of scientific, technical and military subjects. Dissemination of
specialized knowledge was considered essential to achieve scientific
pre-eminence, industrial strength and military superiority, and films
were considered important as teaching aids. To assure the production
of specialized films on various scientific, technical and military
subjects, special studios were established; experts in many fields of
knowledge served as consultants to the film studios. Even the dramatic
film based on fictional scenarios sometimes contained an element of
"science fiction," that is, some link with the world of science, technology and military affairs.

This concern with practical instruction had a political basis.
Communist leaders at the highest levels of the Party and Government

---

[22]Lenin, Stalin partiya o kino, 1938, pp. 31-32.

[23]Quoted by Bella Kashin in The New York Times, October 15, 1933,
Section IX, p. 4.

were interested in the film as a teaching aid on technical subjects.
They repeatedly spoke of motion-picture as an important device for
facilitating scientific, technical and military instruction. A number
of policy statements attributed to Lenin even before 1917 illustrate
this interest in films as a means of practical instruction. During 1914,
in a newspaper article about the "Taylor System" (a method developed by
Frederick William Taylor for improving industrial management) Lenin
noted an important application of motion-picture photography to industrial management:

> The motion-picture is being systematically applied to practical
> instruction of skilled workers, and to raise work tempos, that
> is, to "speed up" the workers more [in capitalist countries].
> For example, the work of a fitter is filmed for an entire day.
> . . . The Taylor System prepares the way for the time when the
> proletariat will take over all socially-useful production and
> will designate its own commission of workers to set correct
> standards and regulations for all socially-useful work.[24]

A few years later, on the eve of the Bolshevik revolution, Lenin commented about the value of films for instruction in the use of new agricultural implements, and also spoke of making films based on nature
studies, to depict the daily activities of wild animals and birds![25]

In 1920, after the Bolshevik revolutionaries had gained the upper
hand in the civil war which had lasted several years, Lenin personally
ordered the production of a special film to disseminate scientific
knowledge to the population. He instructed the Film Department of the
People's Commissariat of Education to prepare, distribute and exhibit a
documentary-style film about a hydraulic machine for mining peat—a

---

[24]Lebedev, Lenin, Stalin partiya o kino, 1938, pp. 8-9.

[25]Ibid., p. 10.

fuel used extensively throughout northwestern Russia, especially in electric-power generating stations. The film "Hydro-Peat" (1920) was the forerunner of many other scientific and technical films produced in the Soviet Union at the request of political leaders.

The Film as "Culture"

Together with such arts as the theater, music, opera and ballet, the motion-picture was defined by Communist leaders as an expression of cultural life in the Soviet Union. Both creative artists and appreciative audiences were expected to look to the film as a manifestation of "socialist culture." The motion-picture was thus to be not only good, and true (by Communist standards), but also beautiful (again, by Communist standards!).

In contrast to Stalin, who was quite opinionated about art, Lenin was somewhat reluctant to define fixed artistic standards, but Lenin very clearly considered films to be important as works of art. Addressing himself to the People's Commissar of Education Lunacharski, Lenin said (in February 1922): "You are reputed to be a patron of the arts, so you must definitely remember that the most important art for us is the film."[26]

Communist leaders continually referred to motion-pictures as an art. For example, a decree signed by Molotov (as chairman of the Council of People's Commissars) in 1933 emphasized that the film was "a factor of cultural growth."[27] Two years later, at the conference convened

---

[26]Ibid., p. 23.   [27]Izvestiya, February 12, 1933.

to mark "the fifteenth anniversary" of the Soviet film industry, the official representative of the Communist Party's Central Committee, Sergei Dinamov, addressed the assembled film producers as follows: "You are responsible for the taste of the millions of people who go to see your films, and if you inoculate them with false beauty, you will be responsible for their loss of taste for real beauty."[28]

Thus creative artists were instructed by Communist leaders to make Soviet films into works of art. The creation of "socialist culture" through the film was also underscored, for example, in a statement by the motion-picture director Friedrich Ermler, himself a Communist Party member since the age of twenty-one; Ermler deftly expressed the "Party line": "We can build a subway in two years, but how sadly lacking in culture are those who build it! Our cinema must aim to develop a new proletarian nobility, to depict the new Socialist man in the making and [to] educate the emotions."[29]

The Film as Ambassador

Because the Soviet film was intended by Communist politicians to be principally a propaganda medium, they did not expect at first that motion-picture exhibitors in "capitalist" countries would show Soviet films to audiences outside the U.S.S.R. Furthermore, Communist leaders must have anticipated that "capitalist" governments would forbid the

---

[28]Dinamov, S., "The Art of Soviet Cinema," International Literature, Moscow, February, 1935, p. 64.

[29]Quoted in Williams, Albert Rhys, The Soviets, New York, Harcourt, Brace, 1937, p. 397.

exhibition of Soviet propaganda films in the "capitalist" countries of
the world. Although the short-lived Communist regimes which temporarily
seized political control in Hungary and parts of Germany (at the time
of the Russian Communist revolution and civil wars) briefly fanned the
flame of international Communist revolution, their rapid downfall frustrated this Communist aim. Consequently for some years the few Soviet
films in existence were exhibited only to audiences in the U.S.S.R.

The international prospects for Soviet motion-picture exhibition
improved, however, as "the international situation" evolved. During
the early 1920's, a Communist-sponsored fund-raising organization called
International Workers' Aid for Soviet Russia was authorized to offer
Soviet films abroad from its Berlin office. A few non-political pictures—films based on pre-revolutionary Russian literary classics and
folk tales—were actually licensed by "capitalist" governments for exhibition. Thus, for example, the Soviet film "Polykushka" (1919) was
exhibited in London during 1924; this tale about a poor Russian serf
was based on a story by the celebrated pre-revolutionary Russian writer
Count Leo Tolstoi, author of War and Peace, Anna Karenina and other
famous literary classics.[30]

Not many Soviet films were licensed by foreign governments, however, and Communist politicians must have realized that the "acceptability" of any particular Soviet film abroad depended not only on the
political relations existing between the U.S.S.R. and other states, but

---

[30]Carter, H., New Theatre and Cinema of Soviet Russia, 1924,
pp. 252-53; Dickinson, T., Soviet Cinema, 1948, pp. 16-19.

also on the political content of the Soviet film in question. Confronted with this fact, Communist leaders lent official support to the export of any Soviet film that would help to build up audiences for Soviet films abroad, and to earn foreign currency (valuta, the Russians called it) for the Soviet government—whether or not such films propagandized openly on behalf of the Communist regime. As a result, the earliest Soviet films exports were not unabashed propaganda pieces praising the Communist regime. Nevertheless, these pictures undoubtedly did build sympathy for Russia and the Russians in the eyes of foreign audiences.

Communist leaders appreciated the fact that a few Soviet films were winning audiences and earning money abroad, but they also began to hope for the day when Communist propaganda films about the "wonderful" life in the Soviet Union and the "evils" of capitalism would be exhibited to foreign audiences. Therefore the politicians encouraged the production of an "intermediate type" of Soviet film containing small doses of propaganda—pictures based on life in the pre-revolutionary Russian empire, but with revolutionary themes. The Russian revolution of 1905— which resulted in a constitutional form of government in Russia twelve years before the Communist seizure of power—was typical of the subject matter of films produced with one eye on the export market. Because of their "proletarian" slant, however, these films on revolutionary themes were not readily accepted in Great Britain, France, or other European countries during the 1920's; government censors in these countries per- mitted private showings by art film appreciation societies, but generally prohibited public exhibition of these films. The policy of the German government was an exception, however. Wider distribution of this type of Soviet film was permitted in that country, and so the Communist regime in the U.S.S.R. was encouraged to persist in its efforts to gain acceptance for Soviet propaganda films abroad. To further the acceptance of "Russian" films in Germany, the Soviet government even permitted some of its creative artists to travel to Germany and to participate in the production of "Russian" films in German film studios!

By 1930, some Communist propaganda films were being exhibited in countries other than Germany—including the United States. After the rise of the Hitler regime, the German market was closed to all Soviet films. The American market became increasingly important. Twenty-nine Soviet films had been exhibited here and there in the United States by 1930, and during the 1930's many other Soviet films were licensed for exhibition in the U.S.A. The Communist politicians in Moscow found another opportunity to earn foreign currency while winning sympathy for Russia, appreciation for "Soviet culture," and friends for the Communist movement. The economic gains were not minimized, either; the Soviet government newspaper Izvestiya pointed out at about this time that films are not merely a matter of ideas or art, but also business—and by business Izvestiya meant "the economic conquest of foreign markets."[31]

During the second world War, some Soviet films were widely exhibited in the United States and Great Britain, but with the onset of "the cold war" in 1946 Soviet films lost the wide distribution they had previously enjoyed in America and England. By this time Communist leaders had begun to export propaganda pictures to Eastern Europe, an area which had

---

[31]Izvestiya, date unknown, quoted in International Review of Educational Cinematography, Volume II, Number 1, January 1930, p. 98.

been "liberated" from German occupation by the Soviet armies. In addition, Soviet films began to penetrate Communist China and some of the nations in Asia, Africa and the Middle East. Communist pictures were exported to India, Indonesia, North Korea, Syria, Egypt and other countries in that part of the world. The Soviet film also penetrated the United Nations organization in 1949, when a documentary picture filmed in Moscow was exhibited at a meeting of the Social Commission of the U. N. Economic and Social Council.[32] In this way the role of ambassador gradually evolved and was added to the other functions which Communist leaders had come to expect of the Soviet film.

The Film as a Source of Income

When Lenin said that films in "capitalist" countries exist chiefly to create profits for the owners of motion-picture enterprises, it became difficult for Communist politicians to define the Soviet film as a source of income without evoking an image parallel to this definition of "capitalist" films. The income-producing potential of film exhibition in the Soviet Union was so great, however, that Communist political leaders could not afford to overlook this source of revenue. Consequently, Communist leaders successively advanced several definitions of the financial role of films in Soviet society in an effort to develop a formula for exploiting the profit-potential, consistent with the propaganda function and the other roles ascribed to the motion-picture.

During the revolutionary days and the civil war period, the ubiquitous shortages of films, electricity and fuel (to heat theaters)

---

[32]*Pravda*, May 18, 1949.

vitiated the revenue-producing potential of films to such an extent
that Communist leaders advocated _free_ film exhibition and did not
trouble themselves extensively with the financial aspect of the motion-
picture. At the beginning of the 1920's, however, Lenin introduced his
"New Economic Policy" to revitalize the economy by means of limited
private enterprise, and he advocated the use of film exhibition profits
to revive the Soviet film industry. Lenin explicitly authorized the
import of foreign films for exhibition in the U.S.S.R. He anticipated
that profits from exhibition of foreign films would go first to revive
the moribund film theaters and distribution offices, but Lenin also de-
creed that at least some of the profits from exhibition in the U.S.S.R.
be used to finance the production of Communist propaganda films. This
stimulus to production was accomplished in two ways: first, film
theaters were instructed to exhibit Soviet propaganda films as a fixed
proportion of their total exhibition schedules, thus creating a "demand"
for such Soviet propaganda films as a by-product of the demand for
foreign entertainment films; second, film production studios in the
U.S.S.R. were obligated to provide the Commissariat of Education with
propaganda films, at no cost to the Soviet government, "to the extent
of ten percent of the total production" of each studio. (As for the
remaining 90 percent of their productive capacity, it was largely devoted to filming "entertainment" pictures designed to rival the foreign
imports--which further increased exhibition profits.)[33]

---

[33]See Lenin's Special Directive to the Deputy People's Commissar of
Education Litkens, dated January 27, 1922, translated in Babitsky,
Soviet Film Industry, pp. 271-72; see also the decree dated January 4,
1922, issued by the Council of Labor and Defense, translated in op. cit.,
pp. 270-71.

As the proceeds from profitable exhibition of foreign films in the
U.S.S.R. mounted, the funds available for production of Soviet films
swelled to such an extent that money was also allocated for the construction of factories to produce movie cameras, projectors and "raw"
film. By the mid-1930's the import of raw film was no longer necessary, and the import of filming and projection equipment was reduced
considerably, owing to Soviet production of these items. During the
1930's, Communist political leaders also allocated some of the exhibition profits to construction of new movie theaters, and to the introduction of the sound-track in Soviet film production and exhibition.

The relatively slow development of the exhibition network, and
the very gradual introduction of sound films throughout the 1930's, lent
support to the theory that proceeds from film exhibition in the U.S.S.R.
were also being allocated by the state to meet expenditures not connected with the motion-picture industry. In other words, a new definition of film function had come into being: the government monopoly was
being used to convert movie admissions—at least in part—into hidden
excise taxes levied on film goers. This coincided with Stalin's reference to "such sources of income as . . . the film." The state had been
collecting revenues from the movie business during the early 1920's,
when movie theaters, having been "nationalized" by the government, were
leased to private individuals as part of the New Economic Policy. By
1924, however, taxes had been reduced—as a matter of Communist Party
policy—to any movie enterprise which failed to earn adequate profits.[34]

[34]See Point 3 of the Section on Motion-Pictures from the Resolution
"On Agitation and Propaganda Work," adopted by the 13th Congress of the
All-Union Communist Party in May 1924, translated in op. cit., pp. 275-76.

From that time on, taxes were leveled not so much against movie enter-
prises, as against the movie-going publics—the urban publics in particular. From the sale of movie tickets the Soviet state obtained funds
not only for the expansion of the film industry, but for various other
purposes.

Summary

Several functions were ascribed to the motion-picture by Communist
political leaders. "Agitation" (i.e., propaganda for the masses) was
the most important raison d'etre for film production and exhibition,
according to the highest political authorities in the U.S.S.R., but other
functions were also defined. These included rivalry with the church and
the vodka trade; dissemination of scientific, technical and military
knowledge; manifestation of cultural activity; communication with foreign
audiences; and accumulation of profits, both inside and outside the
Soviet Union, for the benefit of the Communist Party.

Although the political definition of film functions was elaborated
with the passage of time, the emphasis on propaganda was salient from
the beginning because it reflected the basic social orientation of Communist leaders such as Lenin. Similarly, other groups in the U.S.S.R.—
artists, for instance, and motion-picture audiences—were elaborating
their definitions of film function, starting from definitions which reflected their basic orientations to society and social roles. The
artistic (as opposed to the political) definition of the motion-picture
is the subject of the next chapter.

CHAPTER III

ARTISTIC DEFINITIONS OF THE FILM

Our film art must embody all the old arts--but the old arts by
themselves are not enough. Our art must also be based on Com-
munism--and on a scientific analysis of artistic creativity . . .

We have a powerful Communist weapon in emotion. It is more important for people to react than to be instructed . . .

I wanted to arouse new and fresh emotions in the audience. The
critics of my film were those who think rather than feel . . .

--Sergei Eisenstein, Lecture, 1934

The film artist living in the Soviet Union generally defined the
motion-picture in his own way, relating the film to the artist first of
all. Beyond this, artists usually defined the films in terms similar
to those which Communist political leaders used to delineate the goals
of motion-picture production and exhibition. While the artist's emphasis on the film's relation to himself accounted for most of the conflicts arising between artists and political leaders, those conceptions
of film function which were shared by artists and political leaders paved
the way for reconciliation of divergent opinions.

Although the artist's definition of films in relation to his own
life goals was molded to a considerable extent by his day-to-day participation in film production, artists were by no means the only persons
who enjoyed such continuous contact: some of the political leaders also
had regular contact with the motion-picture, for example, as top-level

administrators and governmental policy-makers in the film industry.
Therefore the unique characteristic of the artist's definition of the
film resulted from a different consideration: devotion to aesthetic
forms of expression. The artist believed in his own creative skill,
and was motivated to express ideas and feelings in a manner that was
not only effective, but pleasing and original as well. This desire to
be creative, original, expressive and pleasing, together with his
involvement in film production, molded the artist's definition of the
motion-picture.

The Primacy of Artistic Expression

To "Western" artists of the early twentieth century, the raison
d'etre was to be found in the expressive originality of their works.
Copy-work was scorned by artists as a mere exercise; material patronage
was justified as a symbolic expression of appreciation by others, because the artist's motive was to create, not to accumulate; lack of
recognition was blamed on an insensitive public. Artists detached themselves altogether from society and lived only for art. "The artist refused to be either an illustrator of social doctrine, a glorifier of the
state, or a producer of consumer goods. He . . . stopped trying to
please a fickle and uneducated public and . . . began pleasing himself
by painting exactly what suited him."[1]

As Tsarist Russia approached a period of war and revolution at the
turn of the century, some Russian artists—especially the painters, sculptors,

---

[1]Kemp, Mary Louise, "Cezanne's Critics," News, The Baltimore Museum
of Art, Volume XXI, Number 2, December 1957, p. 6.

writers, and composers--were steeped in "art for art's sake." Strict
government censorship helped to alienate Russian artists from their
fellow men, as did the failure of those "movements" which had attemped
to raise the educational and cultural level of the Russian peasant
masses.

The Russian theater, ballet and opera differed from other arts,
however, in their great popularity among the urban elite—especially
in St. Petersburg, the capital of Russia. Consequently actors, writers,
directors and scenarists were attracted to the successful theaters.
When the motion-picture industry began to take root in Russia, some of
this talent filtered into the film studios established in Moscow (1908)—
and later Petersburg (1910), Kiev (1915), Odessa (1916) and Yalta (1916).

The first World War stimulated the demand for films produced in
Russia, because imports from France, Germany and the United States were
cut off. Russian film production expanded considerably, and more artists
were attracted to the motion-picture industry. The Russian revolution
of March 1917 may also have stimulated film production briefly, but the
domestic turmoil of 1917, climaxed by the Communist seizure of power in
November, caused some of the successful and famous artists to emigrate.
Such film directors as Buchovetski, Granovski, Turzhanski and Volkov
left Russia to find employment in foreign motion-picture studios, as did
such film actors and actresses as Nikolai Kolin, Ivan Moszhukhin, Nikolai
Rimski, Natalya Kovanko, Zhenia Desni and Natalya Lisenko.[2]

Nevertheless, a number of experienced film artists (like Lev V.
Kuleshov, Olga I. Preobrazhenskaya and Yakov A. Protazanov) remained or

---

[2]Dickinson, T., Soviet Cinema, 1948, pp. 10-11.

returned to Soviet Russia, and the ranks of the film industry were bolstered by the influx of young, artistically inclined people from many walks of life. The young Soviet citizens who became very successful film directors, for example, included an architectural student from the Petrograd Institute of Civil Engineering (Sergei M. Eisenstein), a student of chemistry from Moscow University (Vsevolod I. Pudovkin), a professional boxer (Boris V. Barnet), a repair-man employed by the railroads (Mikhail E. Chiaureli), and a farmer (Aleksander P. Dovzhenko). From diverse backgrounds these people were drawn to art—then to the film industry; the architect Eisenstein became interested in the engineering studies of Leonardo da Vinci and discovered his art; the chemist Pudovkin amused himself by sketching pictures after being captured by the German Army in World War I; railroad repair man Chiaureli dabbled in sculpture and painting as a hobby before he decided to become an actor (and later a film director); the professional boxer Barnet was invited to act in one Soviet film about sports—and decided to become a professional actor; the farm boy Dovzhenko tried his hand at school-teaching, then became a newspaper cartoonist before making a career for himself as a film director.[3]

A number of Soviet directors came from other arts to the film: Lev Arnshtam was a musical director, for example, and Grigori Roshal staged plays before making films—as did Leonid Z. Trauberg, Grigori M. Kozintsev, and Sergei I. Yutkevich.[4]

---

[3]Babitsky and Rimberg, Soviet Film Industry, Appendix III.

[4]Ibid.

To the extent that the creative personnel in the film industry had
a genuine interest in those arts (painting, sculpture, musical composition, etc.) in which opportunities to earn a large income were slight
or non-existent, the motive of personal financial gain must be set aside
in favor of other, more relevant motives. Even in those other arts
(theatre, films, etc.) that can yield a considerable income to the most
talented under present conditions, the motive for personal financial
gain could scarcely have been operative under the conditions which obtained in the Soviet Union immediately after the Communist revolution.
The salaries earned by creative artists during that period were not sig-
nificantly higher than the pay of any working man. Therefore, the
attractiveness of an artistic career--at that time--depended greatly
on the creative inclination of the individual person.

Additional evidence confirms the impression that artistic considerations preoccupied the minds and activities of the film directors employed
in Soviet studios in the years following the Revolution. A great many
film directors put their ideas in print. Numerous articles appeared in
newspapers and magazines, each expressing the opinions of a particular
film director or group of directors. Through the medium of the press,
debates ensued and reflected the development of many schools of thought.
Each of these schools attempted to define the purpose of the film in
Soviet society and to relate this purpose to a particular technique of
film creation. As time went on, these debates attracted attention abroad
and several articles and books published in Western Europe and America
were devoted to a description of these theories of film art. The Soviet
Government, however, stood aside and permitted each school of thought to

publish its views and to create motion pictures in accordance with the theories which the group advocated. Nearly ten years elapsed before the Communist Party began to intervene in these debates, and only then did a rigid policy come into being.

The Communist Party found it possible to stand aside for a decade partly because all of the schools of thought accepted the basic premise that the Soviet film should reflect the triumph of communism and should encourage film audiences to support the Soviet regime. It was evident that "counter-revolutionary" political views would not be tolerated by the state. Therefore, the film artists—particularly the scenario writers and film directors because they had the greatest influence on the content of motion pictures—expressed themselves in terms of artistic considerations. The most important schools of thought were those of Eisenstein, Pudovkin, Vertov, the group headed by Kozintsev, Lev Trauberg, and Yutkevich—who were considered the most radical—and a few others who were slightly more conservative: Dovzhenko, Ermler, Kuleshov, and Protazanov.

Eisenstein was most explicit in his viewpoint and continued to publish his opinions for many years. During the 1930's, he spent considerable time in the classrooms of the Film Institute in Moscow expounding his views. His basic approach was analytic; he sought to discover those artistic principles which would enable him to influence film audiences by playing on their emotions in a calculated manner. His engineering background led him to the view that a scientific analysis of the creation and impact of works of art would lead him to develop a set of techniques by which he could manipulate the emotions of his audiences in the

the desired direction. Although he was not a member of the Communist
Party, his sympathies were clearly with the Bolsheviks and he earnestly
attempted to bring about greater admiration for communism in the spectator. Nevertheless, he considered himself, as an artist, most qualified to analyze the processes of artistic creation and impact—and was
quite dogmatic in expressing his views both in his own films and in debate. Among his best known ideas was the techniques of "montage" and
the principle of the "mass-hero." "Montage" meant the editing of films
to such a degree that the natural sequence of events (as filmed by the
camera) was broken up and completely reconstructed in the editing
laboratory, where Eisenstein spent a great deal of his time; the result
was a film (for instance, "October") which resembled the "stream of
consciousness" novels of James Joyce in discontinuity; in this manner,
Eisenstein bombarded the spectator with a rapidly-changing series of
images in a kaleidoscopic manner, hoping to bring about certain sensa-
tions in the spectator, without much concern for continuity of the
narrative. Similarly, "mass-hero" treatment effaced the individual and
substituted tremendous crowds which moved back and forth across the
screen in great waves of activity. Eisenstein later developed the
theory of "sound counterpoint" (which he announced in print during 1928
in a manifesto also signed by Pudovkin and Aleksandrov)--in which he
proposed to introduce a sound track into the film in such a manner that
the sound would clash with the visual image, rather than synchronizing
picture and sound; thus one more shock was devised by Eisenstein to
batter the emotions of the spectator.[5]

----

[5]Babitsky and Rimberg, Soviet Film Industry, Appendix III.

Pudovkin also developed many theoretical ideas concerning film creation and arranged for the publication of his views in considerable detail. Like Eisenstein, he was of the opinion that the film director is best qualified to judge film content and has the right to impose his ideas on those associated with him in film production. (It has been said of Pudovkin that he forced film actors to go without food or sleep for several days merely to obtain a facial expression corresponding to the tormented image in the director's mind.) Unlike Eisenstein, however, Pudovkin eventually joined the Communist Party--but he retained much of his zeal for independent thought until the end of his life. Although Pudovkin and Eisenstein both won world-wide acclaim, each did so on the basis of his own techniques: Pudovkin depicted typical individuals to represent social groups (such as the workers, the peasants, the army officers, etc. etc.); dramatic impact was achieved by means of extreme situations--episodes of great personal triumph and tragedy. The personal experiences of his heroes and villains always reflected social conditions like war, revolution, famine, colonial exploitation, etc. In these ways, Pudovkin differed from Eisenstein and a strong personal rivalry developed between them, as indicated by the fact that Eisenstein had a dog named Pudovkin and Pudovkin had a dog named Eisenstein.[6]

Of all the Soviet directors, Vertov was most insistent that his example be followed by others. He campaigned tirelessly for the abolition of professional actors in motion picture production. Vertov wrote numerous articles for newspapers and magazines contending that newsreels

---

[6]Ibid. See also Seton, M., Eisenstein, 1952, pp. 91-93.

and documentary films constituted the most acceptable form for Soviet
motion pictures. While both Eisenstein and Pudovkin sometimes used
amateurs in place of professional film actors, Vertov consistently refused to obtain the services of any professional film actor or actress;
furthermore, he spent no time in training or instructing his "cast," but
relied on candid photography devoid of poses or pre-arranged action.
In this manner, Vertov attempted to capture the spontaneity of events
and to dramatize the inherent excitement of human activity.

In 1924, Vertov created a stir by asserting that Lenin himself preferred the documentary film as the medium best suited to the political
education of motion picture audiences in the Soviet Union. Vertov published a quotation from a political directive signed by Lenin to the
effect that the majority of films licensed for exhibition ought to be
pictures devoted to political propaganda rather than entertainment; Vertov insisted that only a documentary film could possibly be classified
as political rather than entertaining! Vertov's views were not generally
accepted at that time, despite the efforts of Vertov and his followers,
and the managing editor of one magazine devoted to film affairs actually
refused to publish Vertov's articles. Nevertheless, by 1928 a movement
was under way among writers generally (in literature, drama, and films)
to inject more realism into Soviet art. As a result of this movement,
which overwhelmed other schools of thought for several years, Vertov's
approach to film making became more widely accepted in the Soviet Union.
Many documentary films were produced between 1928 and 1932 while the output of films with professional actors and synthetic scenery declined.
During the 1930's Vertov's approach was officially criticized as extremist,

but the production of Soviet documentary films continued and reached a
second peak during World War II, when newsreel cameramen photographed
the war in great detail. Although Vertov personally was relegated to
obscurity, he had been very influential in the development of the Soviet
documentary film. Vertov made the documentary film the center of his
life—not merely a cause to be defended, but a program designed to dominate the entire production of motion pictures—and he probably spent as
much time and effort in promoting his ideas as in the actual production
of films.[7]

Another radical approach to films was introduced by a group which
called itself the "Eccentrics." The leaders of this group, which set up
headquarters in Leningrad, were Kozintsev, Lev Trauberg, and Yutkevich.
These "Eccentrics" attempted to destroy the remnants of pre-revolutionary
Russia through ridicule. Their method was strongly influenced by the
circus—which had long been popular in Russia—and the actors in their
films resembled clowns. Their films mocked "bourgeois" society. Realiz-
ing that acid wit and grotesque irony lent themselves best to the destruction of the sacred cows of the pre-revolutionary era, they deliberately chose their subject matter from 19th century life. Their film
about the Paris commune of 1871, which they called the "New Babylon"
(1929), also introduced a good deal of obscure symbolism to the Soviet
screen and caused considerable discussion in the film industry.

Although innovators such as Eisenstein, Pudovkin, Vertov, and the
"Eccentrics" attracted the most attention through their original contributions to film content, they did not fully eclipse the more traditional

---

[7]Dickinson, Soviet Cinema, 1948, p. 22.

school of thought which was rooted in the pre-revolutionary approach to film production both in Russia and other countries. Some of the most talented film directors and scenario writers chose to adhere to the established techniques of plot development, training of actors, and photography—and this group received moral support from such highly placed Soviet officials as the Commissar of Education, Anatol Lunacharski, as well as the majority of film spectators (who were not accustomed to the innovations being introduced by the more radical film directors and scenario writers). In addition, a considerable number of less talented persons in the film industry adhered to the more traditional approach to film making because their creative imagination was somewhat limited. Nevertheless, within the framework of the traditional school of thought there was considerable opportunity for the exercise of creative skill, and a number of Soviet directors and scenario writers produced striking motion pictures—without, however, spending much time in pamphleteering and writing manifestoes.

Dovzhenko poured himself into his creative work and produced several masterpieces. His two greatest artistic contributions, which expressed his inner convictions, were his depiction of the slow-moving peasant at work in primitive villages and immense fields of grain, and also his portrayal of Ukranian folk culture. Like many other talented directors, Dovzhenko frequently wrote his own scenarios and completely dominated the process of film production in Kiev. Unlike most others, he felt a profound sympathy for the passing of the pre-revolutionary style of life and he dared to express this feeling in the face of criticism. Nevertheless, his basic allegiance was to the new Communist

regime and he was willing to modify his viewpoint when it became necessary. Until his artistic freedom was curtailed, he gave powerful expression to the two groups in the Soviet Union which were forced to
accept the inferior status of a minority despite their numerical strength;
the peasants (whose lack of organization undermined their political influence) and the national minorities (who were divided by language,
culture, and geography to such an extent that the Russian culture over-
powered them). The peasants and the national minorities did not give up
without a struggle and the films of Dovzhenko recorded this conflict for
posterity.[8]

Ermler joined the Communist Party as a young man—one of the few
prominent Soviet film directors who chose to do so. By 1919, with his
party membership card in his pocket, he enrolled as a student at the
Petrograd (later Leningrad) Film Institute. During the 1920's he direct ed
several films, of which "Fragment of an Empire" (1929) was considered his
best. Ermler was somewhat addicted to psychological symbolism in his
films and was even accused of admiring Sigmund Freud, but he was considered politically reliable nevertheless and was able to publicise his
opinions through the magazine Proletarskoye kino (Proletarian Film) of
which he became editor. When the Communist Party finally committed itself to a particular point of view concerning the artistic aspects of
film content, Ermler was selected by the Party to produce the film
"Counterplan" (1932), which served as a model—together with "Chapayev"

---

[8]Dickinson, Soviet Cinema, 1948, pp. 31-32.

(1934)--of the approved artistic style dubbed "socialist realism" by
Communist officials in the early 1930's.[9]

Kuleshov introduced another point of view, but hardly a new one,
into the debate over Soviet film art. Kuleshov was the advocate of the
adventure film which had two variants: the detective film and the cowboy film. His "Red detectives" were the counterparts of the heroes of
the American detective films and his heroes on horseback rounded up
cattle and fought the aborigines in a well-known manner. Kuleshov even
transplanted an American to the Soviet Union; his film "The Extraordinary Adventures of Mr. West in the Land of the Bolsheviks" (1924)
featured an American senator and his personal bodyguard--an American
cowboy. Later, Kuleshov produced a movie about the life of the American
writer O'Henry, again reflecting his preoccupation with things American.
Kuleshov's interest in the American style of film making was shared by
many spectators in the Soviet Union, and most of his films were very
popular with Soviet audiences.[10]

Protazanov embodied the pre-revolutionary tradition to the greatest
extent. He had been a Russian film director before the 1917 revolutions
and had supplemented this training by working in west European film
studios for a number of years after that. When he decided to return to
the Soviet Union in 1924, he brought with him the traditional approach
to film making which had been common to western Europe and pre-revolutionary
Russia. By the skillful application of technical "know-how," Protazanov

---

[9]Babitsky and Rimberg, loc. cit.

[10]Ibid., pp. 120-22.

was able to produce dramatic fantasies comparable to lavish foreign
productions--but on the more modest budget required of films produced
in the Soviet Union. Protazanov's greatest triumph was probably his
film "Aelita" (1924), a science fiction drama in which an engineer,
soldier, and detective travel by rocket ship to the planet Mars, wit-
ness a revolution among the inhabitants, and even enjoy a love affair
with the queen of Mars. Protazanov maximized the entertainment side
of films while minimizing political content--but he was always careful
to introduce an element of Communist political doctrine even in the
most fantastic situations (such as the Communist revolution on Mars).
Thus Protazanov represented a point of view about film content far removed from that of the most radical innovators, yet sufficiently propagandistic to meet the minimum requirements of the Communist Party at
that time.[11]

In addition to the men of unusually great talent, there were many
others who directed the production of films in the Soviet Union during
the 1920's. Some had been employed in the pre-revolutionary Russian
movie industry; others found their way into the motion picture industry
after the revolution. A few of the newcomers followed the radical
pioneers like Eisenstein, Vertov, or Trauberg--but most chose to follow
the example of the more conservative film directors such as Kuleshov,
Dovzhenko, or Protazanov.

Although some Soviet films were more experimental than others,
nearly every Soviet motion picture was a departure from the American,
European, or pre-revolutionary Russian motion picture. First of all,

---

[11]Ibid., pp. 119-20.

the subject matter had to meet the minimum requirements of Communist censorship. Second, the film's content generally showed the Communist Party in a favorable light. In addition, some experimentation in the selection and training of actors, in camera work, or in editing, characterized most Soviet films of this period. These experiments reflected the general interest in artistic innovation. Although the most radical innovators conducted the most dramatic artistic experiments, nearly every Soviet director (as well as actors, cameramen, set designers, and scenario writers) were inspired to attempt artistic experiments in the film. Virtually every film director concerned himself with the artistic aspect of the motion picture, and this concern was both a cause and effect of the flair for innovation and experiment that characterized the entire Soviet film industry during the 1920's.

The introduction of the sound film in 1930 opened the door for still greater experiments in film making. As early as 1928, when sound films first made their appearance in America and western Europe, creative artists in the Soviet film industry took a considerable interest in this new development. The film directors Eisenstein, Pudovkin, and Aleksandrov published their manifesto about contrapuntal use of sound in films. When Soviet film directors visited western Europe and the United States in 1929-30, they displayed great curiosity about sound films. Pudovkin began production of the film "Life is beautiful" (1931) with the intention of adding a contrapuntal sound track to this picture. He spent several years in this experiment. Nevertheless, the film was finally released without any sound track. The "official" explanation was that "technical difficulties" had necessitated the release of the film without any sound—but during 1931 a full length dramatic film ("Road to

Life") with a perfectly synchronized sound track was produced in Moscow![12]

Another explanation of Pudovkin's abortive experiment in contrapuntal sound is more congruent with the facts of the situation at that time. The Communist Party had finally endorsed a particular artistic style ("socialist realism") which became obligatory beginning in 1932. One result of this decision was that Party spokesmen gave their support to those films which came closest to the Communist ideal—for example, "Counterplan" (1932) and "Chapayev" (1934). Another result was the suppression of experiments in film production; Pudovkin's innovation in sound may well have been the first victim of the ban against further experiment.

In retrospect, the Party's decision to impose a single artistic form on all Soviet films may have curbed the more extreme artistic innovations which ran counter to the somewhat more conservative trend among film makers. Thus, for instance, Eisenstein's experiments in film editing, and Vertov's insistence on a documentary approach to all film production, and the "Eccentric" group's preoccupation with 19th century subject matter were resisted for the first time by the state which controlled the film industry. But the new policy of the Communist regime not only curbed artistic experimentation—it also injected the opinions of Communist leaders into all matters of artistic style—thereby setting the stage for future conflict between artists preoccupied with creative self-expression and political leaders lacking in artistic knowledge, talent, and experience.

_____

[12]Dickinson, Soviet Cinema, p. 37.

Other Artistic Definitions of the Film

Although artists were concerned foremost with self-expression and expected films to be a vehicle for the artist, they also recognized other functions of the film in Soviet society. In general, the additional components of their total definition of film function paralleled those of the political leaders of the Soviet state.

Some Soviet artists—especially those who became members of the Communist Party—agreed wholeheartedly with Communist leaders on the importance of the propaganda function of the film in society. Most other artists subscribed to this aspect of film function with varying degrees of enthusiasm. A few disagreed, but these individuals had to compromise their principles or retire from participation in the production of motion pictures in Soviet studios.

As for the other functions ascribed to the film—competition with the church and the tavern, dissemination of scientific and military knowledge, manifestation of cultural activity, communication with foreign audiences, and accumulation of profits—all these were accepted to a greater or lesser degree by artists as proper functions for the film in Soviet society.

CHAPTER IV

POPULAR DEFINITIONS OF THE FILM

Throughout the world, motion pictures were produced with the expectation that they would be seen by a large number of spectators.
Pre-revolutionary Russia was no exception. Unlike some of the more
esoteric arts, the motion picture was immediately appreciated by large
audiences in the capital city of St. Petersburg, in Moscow, in Kiev,
and in numerous other cities and towns in the Russian empire. The
rapid development of film production and exhibition in Russia can be
attributed largely to the rapid and widespread acceptance of films by
the millions of spectators concentrated in the major cities and towns.[1]

For many years, the film was in fact limited to the mass spectators
in urbanized areas. The production of specialized films designed for
particular audiences was a later development, made possible by the tremendous success of films produced for the mass market. In addition,
the profits earned in urban exhibition of films paved the way for later
expansion into rural areas--but this development did not take place for
many years. In Russia, particularly, the potential rural audience remained untapped until after the 1917 Revolution, and even then the development of exhibition facilities in rural areas was exceedingly slow

---

[1]Leyda, J., "Prologue to the Russian Film," Hollywood Quarterly,
Volume II, Number 1, October 1946, pp. 35-43.

and by no means comparable to the exhibition network in urban areas
with their greater concentration of population.[2]

The preferences of the urban mass audiences for films played an
important role in the determination of motion picture content, because
attendance at film exhibitions was voluntary everywhere and the financial success of any particular film depended chiefly on the total number of persons willing to spend time and money to see this film.
Although such factors as advertising, opinion leadership, and sheer
habit undoubtedly played a part in the decision "to go or not to go,"
and in the selection of any specific film, the ultimate success of a
motion picture depended on its mass appeal. The tastes and preferences
of urban audiences became increasingly clear as time went by, permit-
ting film producers to gauge the probable success of any proposed film
production in terms of the picture's content. Consequently film industry
officials endeavored to please the public by the selection of popular
stories, settings, "stars," and so on.[3]

The Primacy of the Entertainment Function

When the Communist leaders seized power in the autumn of 1917,
they were confronted with so many problems that the film industry in
Russia could not command their attention. Nevertheless, the average

---

[2]See, for example, the data compiled by Inkeles, from various Soviet
sources. Inkeles, A., Public Opinion in Soviet Russia, Cambridge, Harvard University Press, 1950, p. 301.

[3]This applied to most films exhibited in the Soviet Union, including foreign imports. See, for example, Latitsky, P., Soviet Film
Industry, New York, Frederick A. Praeger, 1955, pp. 68-70.

urban dweller, who had been accustomed to entertaining Russian films
(and foreign pictures, too, until the German blockade cut off the
supply of French and American films) continued to expect that commercial entertainment would be available at local movie theaters. During
the years of civil war that followed, this expectation was repeatedly
frustrated. Movie theaters were damaged in battle, local supplies of
electric power were cut off entirely or diverted for more urgent purposes, fuel was lacking to heat theaters during the long Russian winter,
networks for the distribution of films to theaters deteriorated, and the
depletion of raw film stocks prevented the production of new pictures.[4]
By degrees, the entire motion picture industry came to a virtual standstill. Eventually movie theaters were converted to storehouses or meeting halls; film prints were bootlegged, destroyed, or buried; film audiences were asked to pay a highly inflated price of admission to see the
few films still available.[5] During these years, the movie habit was
thoroughly interrupted for many urban Soviet citizens--but the fascination of motion pictures remained strong nevertheless. As soon as the
import of foreign films resumed (in the early 1920's), theaters began
to re-open and audiences stood in line to buy tickets at the box office.

Some came to the movies merely to keep warm, but most hoped to find
not only warmth but relaxation and entertainment which would enable
them to forget the turmoil which had beset their daily lives.[6]

---

[4]Dickinson, T., Soviet Cinema, London, Falcon Press, 1948, pp. 14-16.

[5]Ibid.

[6]The ex-Soviet scenario writer Martin Lutich confirms the impressions reported by Dickinson, Carter, Harper and other foreign observers.
See Babitsky, P. and M. Lutich, The Soviet Movie Industry, New York,
1953, p. 79.

Exhibitors were quick to sense the mood of their audiences--and of course they had box office receipts to guide them. At first, everything was popular! Films patched together in the most crude manner attracted as many spectators as the slick foreign imports; no one seemed to mind when missing reels disrupted the flow of the film narrative, or when worn-out projectors caused the image to flicker and jump for hour after hour.

Nevertheless, it soon became apparent that the desire for entertainment and amusement and "escape" was still paramount. Foreign pictures, frankly devoted to sheer entertainment (for example "slapstick," cowboy films, detective thrillers, etc.) rapidly drew ahead of the films being produced in Soviet studios. As for the Soviet films--their popularity was inversely proportional to the amount of political content; this was particularly true among those middle-class urban audiences who paid the high prices demanded by commercial exhibitors.[7] The Soviet Government attempted to offset this growing trend by demanding "double-feature" programs which combined a popular entertainment film with a propaganda piece produced in some Soviet studio. When Lenin found time (on January 27, 1922) to address himself to this problem, he dictated a message to the Deputy People's Commissar of Education, Comrade Litkens, as follows: "On every exhibition program a definite proportion ought to be established for a) entertainment pictures for the specific purpose of amusement and income, and b) films of specific propaganda content. . . ."[8]

[7]Harper, S., Civic Training in Soviet Russia, Chicago, 1929, p. 334. See also New York Times, November 7, 1926.

[8]Quoted by Lebedev, N., Lenin, Stalin, partiya o kino (Lenin, Stalin and the Party on the Movie), Moscow, Gosudarstvennoye izdatel'stvo "Iskusstvo," 1938, pp. 19-20.

The Soviet government also experimented with another device for counteracting the growing popularity of entertainment films among urban audiences attending commercial film theaters. The government encouraged the establishment of clubs for the entertainment and political education of workers in the working-class sections of many Russian cities and towns. These clubs were permitted to rent films at extremely low rates and to sell tickets far below the prices paid for commercial movie theater tickets. In return for this price concession, the clubs were expected to exhibit propaganda pictures. In some instances, however, the working-class audiences in these clubs demanded the same entertaining films which were available at higher prices elsewhere.[9] Only in the rural areas and remote regions in eastern Russia did the novelty of films mean so much that the most propagandistic Soviet productions were usually well received. Lenin was aware of this situation and commented on it in the message to Comrade Litkins mentioned above; Lenin urged the Deputy People's Commissar of Education to "pay particular attention to the establishment of movie theaters in the villages and in the East, where they will be novelties, and where, therefore, our propaganda will be especially successful. . . ."[10]

Despite some attempts by the Soviet government to develop film exhibition facilities in rural areas and in the eastern regions of the Soviet Union, the chief source of income from film exhibition throughout the 1920's was the commercial urban movie theater. Only these commercial

---

[9]Harper, op. cit., pp. 331-34.

[10]Lebedev, loc. cit.

theaters charged what the traffic would bear; the price of admission at
a worker's club film show was very low, and film exhibition (by means
of projectors mounted on trucks that went from place to place) in the
rural areas and in the East was generally free of charge to the spectator. The Soviet government decided to permit considerable freedom to
commercial exhibitors, because funds were needed by the state to finance
production in Soviet studios and to develop the exhibition network. In
the directive quoted above, Lenin told Commissar Litkens that "we must
make sure that movie theaters which are in private hands give adequately
of their income to the State as consideration for their lease."[11]

The competition for the film spectator's ruble became fierce under
the conditions of the "New Economic Policy" which restored a considerable
degree of free enterprise to small business. The Northwest Photo—Movie
Administration (Sevzapkino), for example, not only produced and distributed films in the Petrograd (later Leningrad) area, but also expanded
its operations considerably beyond its "territory." Having achieved
tremendous financial success from the exhibit on of films in the former
capital city of Petrograd, this film organization arranged for the lease
of movie theaters in Moscow as well, and even transferred its main distributing office to that city—despite the fact that several other film
organizations were already competing in the Moscow area.[12]

The Soviet government was disturbed by the results of this competition in the field of film exhibition, because the preferences of the
film audience (paying for tickets at commercial film theaters) became

---

[11]Ibid.

[12]Dickinson, Soviet Cinema, pp. 16-18.

paramount in the minds of the film exhibitors--who were concerned chiefly with profits. In November 1927, when the Soviet government celebrated the tenth anniversary of the Bolshevik revolution, Communist leaders were dismayed because the majority of film theaters in Moscow were exhibiting the popular foreign imports instead of the propaganda pictures produced in Soviet studios. Top-ranking officials in the Commissariat of Education decided to review the Soviet film production schedule for 1928--and thirty-six percent of the scenarios previously authorized for production were banned as a result of this review! These officials also issued a statement charging that Sovkino (a stock company established in 1924 to control the distribution of films in the Russian republic of the U.S.S.R.) had pandered to the taste of the philistine--that is, had exhibited those films which audiences wanted to see.[13]

The preferences of film audiences in the Soviet Union were clearly expressed during the 1920's in the most effective way--at the box office. During the 1930's, however, when the Soviet government and the Communist Party undertook a more active role in the motion picture industry, and when Soviet film artists were confronted with more severe demands, the Soviet spectator could no longer exercise as much choice. First of all, the import of foreign films was virtually halted by the Soviet government. Very few foreign productions were exhibited in the U.S.S.R. during the 1930's. Second, the products of Soviet film studios became more heavily saturated with political propaganda;[14] at the same time the

---

[13]Harper, S., Civic Training in Soviet Russia, Chicago, University of Chicago Press, 1929, p. 332.

[14]See Chapter 5.

restrictions on artistic expression reduced the varieties of form and style which had hitherto been available in the spectator. Third, the average Soviet citizen became generally more harassed by the authoritarian regime, through collectivization, extremely rapid industrialization, and the terror of the secret police. Consequently, the average citizen's effort to pit his will against the demands of the regime were seriously undermined, although popular preferences remained important as long as the individual was permitted to decide for himself "to attend or not to attend," while the regime clearly preferred that the Soviet citizen should attend—for the sake of political education and for revenue.

Under these circumstances, Soviet audiences continued to have preferences[15] (not unlike those which they had a decade earlier) and to act on them. Not until the second World War did a change take place: the regime, anxious to win popular support during the crisis, relented and permitted more freedom in the film. At the same time, however, the conflict with the German armies inspired a new surge of patriotism in the Soviet Union and the popular demand for entertaining films gave way—to a certain extent—to a preference for propaganda films which stressed patriotic themes.[16]

After the second World War, the popular interest in entertainment manifested itself once more. Films criticized by the Communist Party for their non-political frivolity proved very successful at the box-office,

---

[15]See Chapter 7.

[16]Golden, N., Motion Picture Markets--1944, Washington, U. S. Department of Commerce, 1944, p. 68.

as did a number of diverting foreign imports. Thus, Soviet film audiences continued to press for entertainment.[17]

Other Definitions of Film Functions

Although the primacy of entertainment can hardly be disputed, film audiences expected the motion picture to be more than merely entertaining.[18] Some persons in the audience enjoyed the propaganda aspect of a film—particularly the nationalistic appeals which glorified Russia (or the Ukraine, or Armenia, or Georgia, and so on)—but also, in some cases, glorification of the "working class," the Communist Parties throughout the world, or political leaders such as Lenin, Stalin, or Kirov.

Some film spectators also wanted films to set moral standards: to condemn drinking, cursing, etc., and to praise good manners, fidelity, courage, and so on. Films also became popular if they supplied the audiences with information about the past, foreign lands, etc., or science, technique, and even military "know-how." Further, some persons in

---

[17]Rimberg, J., "The Soviet Film Industry Today," Quarterly of Film, Radio, and Television, Berkeley, University of California Press, Volume XI, Number 2, Winter 1956, p. 153.

[18]This section is based primarily on a qualitative analysis of interview protocols made available to the writer by Dr. Alex Inkeles of the Russian Research Center at Harvard University—supplemented by other interview records published by the External Research Staff of the U.S. Department of State. American social scientists were able to interview many Soviet citizens who were captured or deported by the Germans during the second World War, or who fled to the West. In 1950, these former Soviet citizens (who feared to return to the U.S.S.R. chiefly because of the harsh treatment which awaited them if they returned) were asked by interviewers to recall their experiences and feelings during the decade before the war. The reliability of these reports has been discussed and established elsewhere in great detail. See, for example, Bauer, Raymond, Alex Inkeles and Clyde Kluckhohn, How the Soviet System Works, Cambridge, Harvard University Press, 1957, pp. 3-15.

the audience looked to the film for artistic inspiration: truly beautiful scenes or costumes, inspired acting, moving stories that would take
their place among the greatest works of literature and art, and so on.
In this connection, some looked to the film to reproduce artistic masterpieces created for other media such as the novel, the stage, or the opera
house.

Even those who fled from the Soviet Union during the 1940's are not
averse to making favorable comments about Soviet films. The evidence
suggests that most Soviet citizens who left the U.S.S.R. in the 1940's
had been deeply absorbed in the day-to-day aspects of Soviet life during
the 1930's, in the same uncritical manner in which most citizens accept
social institutions and conventions of the society in which they live.

Quite a few Soviet citizens are ardent film "fans." For instance,
one young man reports that "I did not let a single film go by without
seeing it." This individual, who had been imprisoned in the Soviet Union
during the 1930's, nevertheless enjoyed Soviet films so much that he
tried to see them all. It should be added, however, that his father
had once been a member of the Communist Party--but was expelled during
the 1930's and disappeared. This same young man, who was a truck driver
by occupation, and had once been a member of the Communist Youth Organization (Komsomol), also said that he considered Soviet films true-to-
life, ". . . and even now [in 1950, in Germany] I take them for the real
stuff."[19]

---

[19]Personal Interview No. 417, Project on the Soviet Social System,
Russian Research Center, Harvard University.

Many Soviet citizens liked motion pictures unless some specific episode or fact depicted in the film contradicted the individual's personal knowledge and experience. Therefore, Soviet films about the historic past or about foreign countries were widely accepted and appreciated—since the spectator had no way of evaluating the truthfulness of these films, except to compare them with other Soviet sources of information about the past or about life abroad. Thus, one former Soviet citizen reported that he considered historical films true-to-life and suitable for exhibition ". . . even after the overthrow of Bolshevism." This respondent, who had been a professional army officer, once belonged to the Communist Party.[20] Another person, who had been expelled from the Komsomol and had been arrested for breach of discipline at a military school, reported that "historical films did not distort the facts, although the central character (for example, Tsar Peter the Great) was depicted in the light of current policies."[21] Another young man, who had been a Komsomol member and had served six years in the armed forces of the Soviet Union after completing the equivalent of a high school education, said: "On the basis of my studies about Russian history, I feel that Soviet films are objective."[22] Another young man, who was in a trade school when the war began in 1941, reported that "in every film, things are made to look attractive—but in general Soviet films were true-to-life."[23] Another professional army officer, who had taken

---

[20]Personal Interview No. 136.   [21]Personal Interview No. 240.
[22]Personal Interview No. 641.   [23]Personal Interview No. 378.

courses in automobile maintenance and had been through an artillery school before the war, said he "accepted historical films as essentially correct, but was more skeptical of films depicting contemporary Soviet life." This soldier was captured twice by the German armies but escaped to rejoin the Soviet armed forces—and also fought with a detachment of Russian "partisans" behind the German lines.[24]

Some Soviet citizens, who had generally accepted the Soviet way of life, looked to motion pictures as an additional source of information about the "Party line" in matters of politics, morality, and so on. Thus, one teacher reports that she felt obliged to go to the movies regularly just because Soviet films had "ideological significance." This woman, who was teaching Russian language and literature in an elementary school during the late 1930's, said she "had to tell my pupils why they should go to see a particular film."[25] Another school teacher, whose father had also been a school teacher, reported that "as a teacher, I considered it my duty to see political pictures."[26]

The uncritical acceptance of films was readily admitted by a number of persons, and undoubtedly many others did the same while they lived in the Soviet Union. A young woman, who happened to be a nurse in a large Ukrainian city, commented that "we enjoyed Soviet films for their humor and we never looked at them critically."[27] Another nurse, now living in the United States, reported that Soviet films were superior to American films: "In general, I think that Soviet movies were better than the ones in the United States. They were better from the technical

---

[24]Personal Interview No. 445.

[25]Personal Interview No. 91.

[26]Personal Interview No. 493.

[27]Personal Interview No. 642.

standpoint, and I found their subjects more interesting to me."[28] Another
respondent, who fled from the Soviet Union after the end of the second
World War, also liked the Soviet films produced during the 1930's and
did not criticize them. He reported that Soviet films produced _after_
the second World War were "cheap propaganda, and people are dissatisfied
with them, but pictures made before the war were interesting; there was
no propaganda in them."[29]

Some of the persons interviewed were quick to point out that Soviet
films had won international recognition. This thinly disguised patriotism is revealed, for instance, in one comment by a young man who had
operated a tractor on the collective farms: "The Russians won some
prizes for their films abroad."[30] Another respondent, a young man from
the Ukraine who was captured by the German army in 1941, said that
"Soviet films, even propaganda films, were better than films made in the
West. The Soviet films had to be interesting just because they contained
propaganda."[31] Another uncritical view was expressed by an old man, a
locomotive engineer, who said he was tired of politics and "just went
to the movies to relax. I was not interested in the propaganda."[32] An
electronics expert who did not leave the Soviet Union until after the
end of the second World War--and who had been a field grade officer in
the Soviet army--said that "in general, the movies are a very desirable
way of spending time, although there is too much repetition of certain

---

[28]Personal Interview No. 1124. [29]Personal Interview No. 144.
[30]Personal Interview No. 336. [31]Personal Interview No. 398.
[32]Personal Interview No. 492.

themes in them."[33] Another elementary school teacher and part-time
journalist admitted he had been uncritical. "I perceived Soviet films
emotionally," he said when interviewed in the United States in 1950.[34]
Another young Soviet citizen interviewed in the United States said:
"When it came to Soviet films, my attitude was childish."[35]

Many persons liked certain types of films better than others.
Historical films were popular with many who avoided films on contemporary
subjects. A mechanic, interviewed in New York, put it this way: "As
Soviet films were political and as I was tired of politics, I avoided
Soviet films—except the historical ones."[36] Another former Soviet
citizen said that he "accepted historical films as true-to-life, but was
skeptical of pictures on contemporary subjects."[37] Another woman, who
had been a bookkeeper in the Soviet Union, said that she liked some of
the historical films.[38] An engineer employed in a rural area near
Moscow reported that "Soviet films on historical subjects were excellent."[39] A number of other persons said they preferred films on historical topics.

Other types of films also created favorable impressions. A bookkeeper in the fur industry said, "There were some good Soviet musical
films."[40] A man who worked as an inspector in the Ministry of Trade
noted that "films with Russian songs were popular."[41] Another young

------

[33]Personal Interview No. 522.   [34]Personal Interview No. 1204.

[35]Personal Interview No. 1507. [36]Personal Interview No. 1593.

[37]Personal Interview No. 445.   [38]Personal Interview No. 1108.

[39]Personal Interview No. 473.   [40]Personal Interview No. 302.

[41]Personal Interview No. 381.

man, who had studied aircraft construction and who later became a Soviet agent in Austria until he defected in 1947, said he found ordinary movies uninteresting but "I liked to see the newsreels."[42] A young man who had worked on a collective farm reported that "some Soviet films depicted young people and their love affairs. You could believe that, but you could not believe the propaganda films."[43] A woman journalist from the Ukraine was partial to film versions of Russian literary works.[44] A sports instructor and Komsomol official agreed, saying that "films based on literary classics were successful because they were genuine—but political films were failures because they were neither true-to-life nor artistic."[45]

Those who agreed with the typist from the town of Simferopol that Soviet films were not entertaining and did not allow the spectators to "forget themselves"[46] sometimes went to see the foreign films being exhibited in the Soviet Union. A bacteriologist (whose husband was a professor of biology) said: "We could relax when we saw foreign films."[47] An administrative official in the Ministry of Trade, who was commissioned a field grade officer in the Army Quartermaster Corps during the war, reported that he "always saw foreign films twice."[48] A man who had started his career as a common laborer but became a teacher of mathematics said that "we tried to catch a glimpse of life in the West by

---

[42] Personal Interview No. 301.   [43] Personal Interview No. 116.

[44] Personal Interview No. 644.   [45] Personal Interview No. 189.

[46] Personal Interview No. 1368.   [47] Personal Interview No. 373.

[48] Personal Interview No. 381.

seeing foreign films. We wanted to experience the joy of individual
freedom. Coming home from a foreign film, we always said to each
other: 'How good life must be there.' We lacked a critical attitude
to foreign films—even when we should have been a bit sceptical!"[49]

Thus Soviet citizens commented on their preferences in films.[50]
Attitudes to the political content of the motion picture varied considerably; different citizens expressed enthusiasm, or passive acceptance, or hostile rejection—but all of them seem to agree that the
individual spectator is entitled to have a preference and to exercise
his right "to go or not to go." The collective result of these millions
of individual decisions played a significant role in the determination
of film content. The public's desires were measured daily at the box
offices all over the Soviet Union.

[49]Personal Interview No. 54.

[50]Some quantitative measurements of attendance frequencies and
audience preferences are presented in Chapter 7.

PART III

POWER RELATIONSHIPS IN THE SOVIET FILM INDUSTRY:

THE PARTY, THE ARTISTS AND THE AUDIENCES

CHAPTER V

THE POWER OF THE COMMUNIST PARTY

The power of the Communist Party over the Soviet film industry
has frequently been asserted and never questioned. Through the Party's
control over the Soviet government (including the administration of the
film industry), over the associations of artists and workers (including
trade unions) and over individuals, the Party has always been in a position to exert maximum pressure to bring about the achievement of its
aims.

In the motion picture industry, the Party has taken responsibility
for approving all major personnel appointments, approving all production plans and schedules, reviewing all films at each stage (from
scenario to final preview of the completed picture) and formulating
policies for the distribution—including import and export—and exhibition of films. The Party has also recruited into its ranks most administrators employed in the film industry and a number of artists as well.
Thus the Party appeared to be in full control of the Soviet film during
the entire period of its dominance in the Soviet Union.

In the conflict of interests between the Party, the artists and
the audiences, there were some instances in which the Party dramatically
asserted its power. Thus, for example, some completed films were banned
by the Communist Party. In the day-to-day operations of the motion
picture industry, however, the Party's role was generally not so dramatic,

decisive, or well publicized; nevertheless, these continuing regulatory activities by the Party were also of great importance to the Soviet film industry.

In view of the power of artists and audiences, however, the extent of the Party's influence on film content should not be exaggerated. An analysis of film content (see below) that measures the degree of propaganda in Soviet films reveals that the Party continued to compromise in most day-to-day decisions regarding film content and enjoyed only limited success in its efforts to increase the propaganda content of films over the years. Thus a measurement of propaganda content indicates clearly the limited ability of the Party to permeate Soviet films with political propaganda.

The Measurement of Propaganda Content

The method developed for purposes of this research study is based on techniques developed by Harold Lasswell, Daniel Lerner, and others.

Elements of Propaganda Content

Several criteria had to be met in the development of this research method for measuring propaganda content. The aspects of content to be measured had to be clearly related to the propaganda aims of the Communist Party. Further, they had to be sufficiently objective so that personal judgment was held to a minimum and subsequent analysis would yield essentially the same results whether repeated by this analyst or others. In addition, the dimensions of the analysis had to be suitable for use despite the paucity of information about the content of many of the Soviet films catalogued and studied. Finally, the method had to be based on a logical and convenient unit of study, namely, the individual film; this meant that the elements of content designated as measures of propaganda content had to be constant for any particular film. The technique developed for this analysis meets these criteria quite well.

Three elements of film content were selected as indicators of the extent of propaganda in a Soviet motion picture. One of these elements is the time period when the action takes place. Another element is the Communist affiliation of the principal character who resolves the problem presented in the film; in the absence of a successful resolution of the problem, the principal victim of the problem is substituted. The third element is the main problem itself—and the extent to which "social" problems are resolved in a manner acceptable to the Communist Party line at any given moment.[1]

Each of the three elements measured is clearly related to the propaganda aims of the Communist Party. As regards the time period, the objective of the Party has been (and continues to be) that propaganda must concern contemporary topics. The Party repeatedly demands more films on contemporary subjects, because current problems and solutions can best be illustrated by means of contemporary subject matter; in addition, the contemporary audience can most readily identify with contemporary characters and situations. As regards the Communist affiliation of the central character (who resolves the main problem), the Party has regularly insisted that the officials and members of the Communist Party are best equipped to deal with political and social problems. The Party has always wanted to depict its leaders as superior beings and its members as the elite of human society. Thus the propaganda interests

[1]Concerning the interdependence of these three variables, see the Appendix.

of the Party are best served by assigning the role of the "problem solver" to the alleged problem-solvers of the Communist society--the leaders of the Party. As regards the main problem and its resolution, the Party has always demanded that "social" problems must be emphasized in works of propaganda. It is the social problem, not the personal problem, that is important to human society and of particular importance to a society whose leaders are concerned with social change. Thus, personal problems lacking social implications are of no particular interest to the Party in its formulation of propaganda policies; only social problems are significant and suitable topics for the artist in Soviet society. Furthermore, the Party demands that social problems be resolved in accordance with the Party line. Therefore the absence of a solution (or a non-Communist solution) of any given social problem is contrary to the propaganda aims of the party. The exact nature of the social problem may vary from time to time as conditions change, but social problems that are unique to the Communist party (for example, membership in the Communist Party, or loyalty of Party members to their leaders) are of particular significance because they bear on the unique character of the elite in the Communist world.

The three elements used in this content analysis are also sufficiently objective so that the personal judgment of the analyst is held to a minimum. The time period is generally identified with sufficient clarity to permit a precise rating. The political affiliation of the "problem-solving" hero is also made clear in most Soviet films. As for the main problem and its resolution, some judgment is generally involved, but the tendentious nature of most Soviet films facilitates an objective judgment of the social nature of the main problem, and the extent to which the resolution of this problem is in accord with the Party line.

Despite many gaps in the available information about the content of Soviet films, most summaries of film plots included information about all the three elements measured: the time period, the political affiliation of the hero "problem-solver," and the main problem and its resolution. Whenever any of these elements were not sufficiently described to permit a rating to be made, the missing element was omitted altogether and the film was judged only on the basis of the other two available content elements.

Each of the three elements used as a basis for measuring the extent of propaganda content in a given film remained constant throughout the film and coincided with the unitary approach to each film. Thus every film was set in a specified time period. (A few films covered an unusually long time span—longer than any one category used in the ratings—but the most recent time period depicted in the film was systematically used as the basis for a rating; thus a film which begins its story many years ago but ends in a contemporary period was considered a contemporary film.) Each film had one—and only one heroic "problem-solver"—a central character who brings about the resolution of the principal problem. (Again, a few films were exceptional in this regard, insofar as a problem was solved "collectively" by a group of heroes, but in these cases the political affiliation of the highest-ranking member in the group was used as the basis for a rating.) As for the main problem and its resolution, virtually all films had but one main problem and one resolution of the problem. (In the few cases where several problems were depicted in a single film, the problem selected for a rating was the one depicted

as the most important or the one most strongly emphasized by the Party
line at that particular period. When more than one resolution to a
problem was depicted, the resolution most congenial to the current
Party line was selected as the basis for a rating.) Therefore the three
elements selected as measures of propaganda content generally could be
rated in a unitary manner coordinate with tne film unit, but in border-
line cases the propagandistic intent was assumed and the rating was
systematically selected to maximize the propaganda content of the particular film in question.

Rating Scales

The time periods depicted in Soviet films were classified according
to the following ratings:

Rating	Time Period
Six	0-5 years ago
Five	6-10 years ago
Four	11-25 years ago
Three	26-40 years ago
Two	41-100 years ago
One	More than 100 years ago

This rating system distinguishes between contemporary subject matter and
other subject matter, with greater weight assigned to the more contemporary subjects. Fairy tales were classified as having taken place more
than 100 years ago. The small number of films with futuristic settings
were assigned a rating of Six.

The Communist affiliation of the "problem-solving" hero was classified according to the following ratings:

Rating	Affiliation
Six	Chief of the Communist Party
Five	National Officer of the Communist Party
Four	Local Official of the Communist Party
Three	Rank-and-file member of the Communist Party
Two	Rank-and-file member of the Komsomol
One	Not a Komsomol or Party member

This rating system distinguishes between degrees of Communist affiliation, with greater weight assigned to the more intensive degrees of affiliation. Political commissars in the armed forces were rated the same as local officials of the Communist Party. Members of the Pioneer organization were rated One because of their extreme youth and the popular (not elite) character of membership in this organization.

The main problem and its resolution was classified according to the following ratings:

Rating	Problem and Resolution
Six	Communist Party Problem and Communist Party Resolution
Five	Social Problem and Communist Resolution
Four	Social Problem and "Progressive" Resolution
Three	Social Problem and other Resolution
Two	Social Problem: No Resolution
One	No Social Problem

Problems pertaining to Communist Party membership, loyalty, or discipline were rated Six. The presence or absence of social values (laws, mores, or commonly-accepted expectations) provided the basis for distinguishing between social and non-social problems; personal problems without social implications—e.g., should the hero marry the beautiful brunette or the beautiful blonde?—were assigned a rating of One.

As regards the resolution of problems, a "Communist resolution" could take place only when the "Party line" was known to the hero and was applicable to the problem. Communist solutions could be chosen by persons who were not members of the Communist Party or Komsomol, however; the hero had only to be familiar with the Communist "line" applicable to his problem.

Solutions to social problems were classified as "progressive" if the action was taken by someone not acquainted with the Party line—provided that the Party subsequently defined this action as the correct one under the circumstances. For example, Alexander Nevski made a "progressive" decision hundreds of years ago when he led the armies of Novgorod against the Teutonic Knights—according to the Communist Party line in the year 1938, when the film biography of Nevski was released.

"Other resolutions" of social problems were those not approved by the Communist Party; in this category fall religious solutions to social problems (even after the Party came to terms with the Russian Orthodox Church), or pacifist attitudes during the "Great Patriotic War" against Germany in the 1940's, or "cosmopolitan" internationalism and humanism during the period of the "cold war" against the West in the late 1940's.

Results

Time Period

The results of the analysis of time periods (depicted in films) are presented graphically on the next page. The higher the rating, the more contemporary was the subject matter of those films. On the basis of

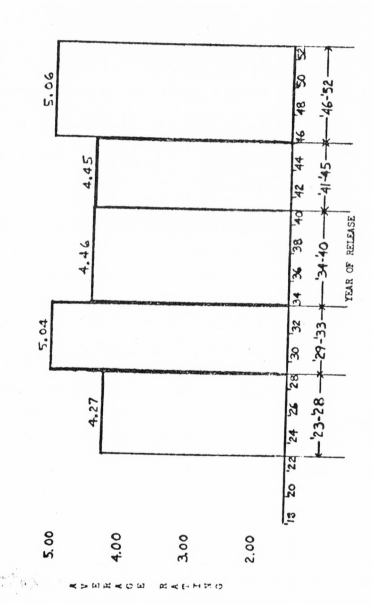

TIME PERIODS DEPICTED IN SOVIET FILMS:
A Propaganda Content Analysis

available information, ratings were made on approximately 500 motion pictures.

The average rating is charted for each of five time divisions of the Soviet era, too, according to the date of release of each film. Thus it is possible to compare the average rating for films released between 1923 and 1928 with the average rating for films released between 1929 and 1933, and so on. At least 50 pictures were rated in each of the five time divisions of the Soviet era prior to the death of Stalin.

The data indicate that many Soviet films have a contemporary setting. Films with non-contemporary settings were most prevalent among pictures released during the period 1923-1928, but more than one-third of even these films had a contemporary setting. Among films released between 1929-1933, more than one-half had a contemporary setting and the average rating is correspondingly higher, as indicated on the chart. This means that the Communist Party enjoyed some success in its efforts to increase the proportion of films on contemporary subjects at the time of the introduction of the first Five-Year-Plan. Motion pictures released between 1934 and 1940 reveal a trend in the opposite direction, however, as the proportion of films with non-contemporary subject matter increased, thereby lowering the average rating for films released during the period 1934-1940. Approximately one-half of these films were on contemporary subjects.

Although the proportion of war-time films (released between 1941-1945) on contemporary subjects increased, the average rating for war-time films remained at the same level as the average rating for the pre-war films because of a corresponding increase in the proportion of films on historical subjects going back a century or more. Thus the

average rating remained constant for more than ten years, from 1934 to
1945. In the post-war era (1946-1952), as the Communist Party again
stridently demanded films on contemporary subjects, two-thirds of all
films released had contemporary settings, so that the average rating
for the post-war period increased over the two previous periods and even
exceeded the period of the first Five-Year-Plan.

In summary, Party demands for contemporary subject matter in films
met with some success when these demands were most intense, that is,
during the period of the first Five-Year-Plan (1929-1933) and the post-
war era (1946-1952).

Communist Affiliation of the Problem-Solving Hero

In general, the hero credited with the solution of the film's problem was not even a rank-and-file member of the Communist Party. As indicated on the chart that follows (see next page) the average rating on
a scale from One to Six was much lower for this element of propaganda
content than for the element previously discussed. Men not affiliated
with the Party were frequently credited with heroism and wisdom in Soviet
films and members of the Komsomol appeared more frequently than members
of the Communist Party.

During the period 1923-1928 many films depicted ordinary Russian
people as victims of the "evils" of capitalism or feudalism in Tsarist
Russia. (As these films lacked positive heroes, the political allegiance
of the principal victim in each film was made the basis for a rating,
on the assumption that films depicting Communist Party revolutionaries
victimized by the Tsarist regime contained a greater degree of Communist
propaganda than pictures which showed ordinary Russian citizens as

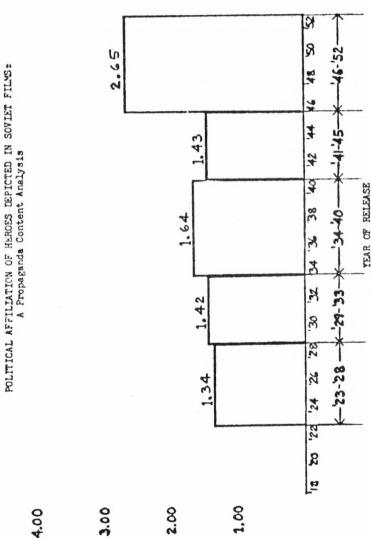

POLITICAL AFFILIATION OF HEROES DEPICTED IN SOVIET FILMS:
A Propaganda Content Analysis

victims of the Tsarist regime.) Most other films released between
1923 and 1928 depicted ordinary Russian people in heroic proportion,
but virtually no attempt was made to portray members of the Communist
Party as an elite.

During the next two periods (1929-1933 and 1934-1940) there was a
trend toward greater glorification of the Party as the leader and
"problem-solver" in human affairs. Only one film (Eisenstein's "October") released during the 1920's depicted the leaders of the Communist
Party, but several such films appeared after 1936. Consequently the
average rating for films released between 1934 and 1940 is somewhat
higher, but the number of films about Lenin, Stalin and others of high
rank in the Party was small during the 1930's in comparison to the total
number of films released during that decade.

With the advent of World War II, the ordinary Soviet citizen again
received most of the credit for heroism and wisdom in Soviet films.
The average rating for films released between 1941 and 1945 declined
from that of the previous period. Only towards the end of the war did
some Soviet films depict Communist Party officials in heroic proportions;
nearly nine-tenths of war-time films, however, had non-Party, non-Komsomol
heroes and heroines.

The proportion of non-Party, non-Komsomol heroes and heroines was
considerably reduced during the post-war period as the Communist Party
demanded greater credit for its role in the conduct of the war and other
affairs. Many post-war films credited Stalin personally with unlimited
wisdom and depicted him as the heroic problem-solver. Consequently,
the average rating for films released between 1946 and 1952 was very

much higher than the average for any previous period. Those films which
did not depict Stalin did give credit to Communist Party officials—
particularly local Party secretaries—and portrayed these Party officials as heroes. It should be noted, however, that there were virtually
no Komsomol heroes in the post-war films and that three-fifths of the
post-war films had non-Party, non-Komsomol heroes.

To summarize, ordinary men and women without Party affiliation predominated among heroes in Soviet films at all times. Not until the
post-war era was there a considerable increase in the proportion of
heroes depicted as being affiliated with the Party.

Problems and their Resolution

Only one percent of more than 500 films were found to deal with
Communist Party affairs such as Party membership or discipline, and most
of these were released between 1934 and 1940—the time of the purges.
However, most films dealt with social problems and depicted a Communist
resolution of the problem (rank Five).

The average rating of the early Soviet films (released between
1923 and 1928) was somewhat lower than the average for films released
in later years (see next page). During the period of the first Five-
Year-Plan, when the Party greatly strengthened its demand for more
political propaganda in films, the average rating increased considerably,
indicating that social problems and Communist solutions were being made
the subject matter in a higher proportion of Soviet films.

Films that were released between 1934 and 1940 had a lower average
rating, as the political pressure eased. (Stalin had promised after the

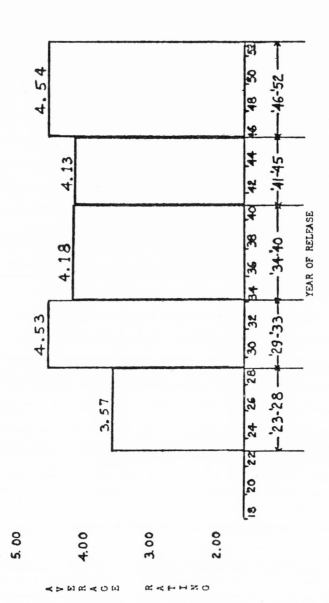

PROBLEMS AND SOLUTIONS DEPICTED IN SOVIET FILMS:
A Propaganda Content Analysis

end of the first Five-Year-Plan that life would become more pleasant.)
During the war years, too, there was somewhat less pressure for extensive propaganda, as reflected in the rating for the period 1941-1945.
At the war's end, however, the Party again called for more propaganda
in films, as indicated by the higher rating for the average film released between 1946 and 1952. Whereas two-fifths of the early Soviet
films depicted social problems and Communist solutions, four-fifths
of the post-war films contained subject matter of this kind.

In summary, most Soviet films featured social problems and Communist solutions, but this choice of subject matter was particularly
pronounced during the period of the first Five-Year-Plan (1929-1933)
and in the post-war era (1946-1952).

Composite Ratings of Propaganda Content

A combination of the three distinct elements (ratings of the time
period, the political affiliation of the hero, and the problem and its
resolution) provides a more comprehensive measure of the degree of
propaganda content in Soviet films. The combined ratings are depicted
on the next page. They provide a convenient summary of the measures
previously discussed.

The combined average for the films released between 1923 and 1928
indicates that they were by no means devoid of propaganda content.
Nevertheless these early Soviet films contained somewhat less propaganda
than pictures released in subsequent years, as measured by the composite
rating.

TIME PERIODS, POLITICAL AFFILIATION OF HEROES, PROBLEMS AND SOLUTIONS:
A Composite Measure of Propaganda Content

15.00

12.00

9.00

6.00

3.00

9.18

10.99

10.28

10.01

12.25

(3.57)   (4.53)   (4.18)   (4.13)   (4.54)

(1.34)   (1.42)   (1.64)   (1.43)   (2.65)

(4.27)   (5.04)   (4.46)   (4.45)   (5.06)

'18 '20 '22 '24 '26 '28 '30 '32 '34 '36 '38 '40 '42 '44 '46 '48 '50 '52

'23-28   '29-33   '34-40   '41-45   '46-52

YEAR OF RELEASE

In response to the Party's demand for more propaganda content, film makers released motion pictures during the period 1929-1933 with a higher average rating. Although the Party would have been pleased to maintain the same level of propaganda content during the next period (1934-1940), film artists were dissatisfied with Party demands and their objections were reflected in a decline in the average composite rating for this period. The artists continued to assert themselves during the war years and were able to reduce the propaganda content once more, as measured by the rating for the period 1941-1945.

The Communist Party reasserted itself in the post-war period and insisted on higher levels of propaganda content in films. The relentless political pressure resulted in a distinct increase in propaganda content during the period 1946-1952, as reflected in the composite rating for this period—the highest for any period under study. Thus, despite steady resistance by the artists and despite extensive set-backs in Party efforts to raise propaganda content all the time, the Communist Party seemed to be making definite progress in the achievement of its aims during the last years of the Stalin era, so far as film content is concerned.

Comparison of Propaganda Content and Film Production

Analysis of Soviet film content and the volume of production for the period 1923-1952 (see p. 108) indicates that the volume of production fluctuated considerably. The content of films, on the other hand, always reveals the presence of all three elements: politics, art and entertainment. This does not mean that the content was uniform throughout this period in every respect, but rather that the three content elements--propaganda, art and entertainment--were to be found in films produced in Soviet studios, despite changes in the propaganda line of the Communist Party. Efforts by the Party to increase the propaganda component were resisted by both artists and audiences with the result that production and attendance declined each time the Party made another attempt to increase the amount of propaganda at the expense of artistic content or entertainment content in an individual film or in the total output of the motion picture industry.

The fluctuations in the annual volume of production of feature films are quite clear--despite the contradictions to be found in published data about Soviet film production. An analysis of the date of production of approximately 750 films (constituting between 65 and 85 percent of the estimated total volume) reveals the trends from year to year and from period to period. Whatever inaccuracies may exist in this analysis--due to the fact that it is based on a sample rather than a total--the trend during each of several time periods must correspond to reality within a small margin of error, because the films included in the sample were not selected with any known bias; rather they are included because information (title, director, studio, year of release) was published in at least one of the many books or articles studied for the purpose of compiling this information over a period of ten years. There is no doubt that the compilation includes all major feature films and most of the lesser-known pictures as well--particularly those released by the major studios in Moscow and Leningrad. The films not included in the compilation probably include those pictures which were banned (and expunged from official records) as well as a number of

productions released by the smaller studios which produced films intended for limited audiences, such as the national minorities, or
children, or selected occupational groups such as railroad men, miners,
or members of the armed forces. Thus, the film titles not included in
the compilation are chiefly pictures of secondary significance from the
standpoint of an analysis of the major output of Soviet film studios.

The chart on the following page depicts the approximate number of
films released each year from 1918 to 1952. The time periods mentioned
in the course of this chapter are well suited to an analysis of the
chart. They are: 1918-1922, 1923-1928, 1929-1933, 1934-1940, 1941-
1945, 1946-1952.

Note that more than 20 films were released during the year 1918,
whereas less than 20 films were released in each year from 1947 to 1952.
Other trends depicted on the chart can be summarized as follows: The
period 1918-1922 shows a continuous decline in the volume of production,
caused by the Civil War in general and by the shortage of raw film stock
in particular. The period 1923-1928 is one of steady increases in the
volume of production—part of the general recovery which took place as
a result of the so-called "New Economic Policy"—at a time when artistic
experiments were at least tolerated. The period 1929-1933 shows a steady
decline, as the first Five-Year-Plan dominates Soviet life. The period
1934-1940, after overcoming the low point reached in 1933, is characterized by erratic fluctuations in film production, ranging from 18 to
27 pictures a year—as extensive purges take place. In the period 1941-
1945, there is an increase in the volume of production in the first year
of the war (1942) and a slight decline in the war years that follow.

108

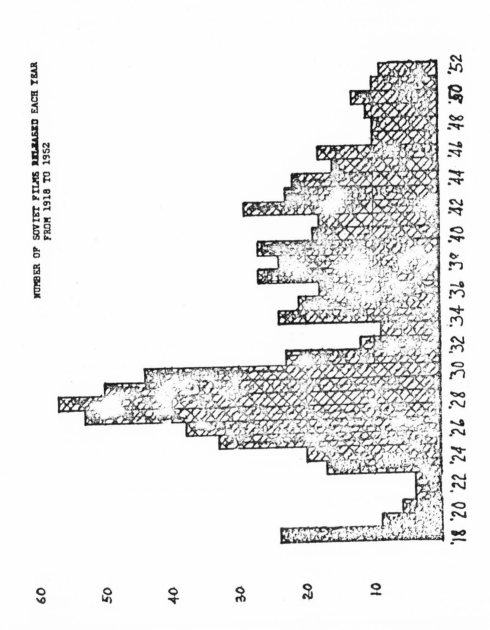

NUMBER OF SOVIET FILMS RELEASED EACH YEAR
FROM 1918 TO 1952

The period 1946-1952 is characterized by a sharp decline (in 1947) which levels off—so that the average annual volume of production is approximately ten films a year for a period of six years. It is therefore evident that in the periods when the call for propaganda is very loud and strident (1929-1933 and 1946-1952), the volume of production declines in dramatic fashion.

The weakness of Communist efforts to use the motion picture industry as a vehicle for propaganda purposes becomes apparent when film content is re-examined against the background of film production. Whether Communist achievements in the area of film content be considered large or small, it is clear that the Party lost ground with respect to film production whenever it seemed to be gaining in its efforts to control film content. Thus, the resistance manifested in the industry by film artists assumed different forms: sometimes the artists tried to reduce the propaganda content in films, and sometimes they interrupted the flow of films from Soviet studios.[2]

A comparison of propaganda content and film production (see next page) for each of several periods dramatically reveals the inverse relationship between propaganda content and film production. A comparison of the period 1923-1928 with the period 1929-1933 shows that production went down and propaganda increased. A comparison of 1929-1933 with the next two periods (1934-1940 and 1941-1945) reveals the opposite trend, consistent with the inverse relationship: production increased while propaganda declined. Finally, a comparison of the two periods from 1934 to 1945 with the period 1946-1952 again shows the same inverse relation: an increase in propaganda content and a decline in production.

---

[2]Interruptions were caused by delays and absences resulting from fear, mental torpor or police action, and sometimes from premeditated opposition.

110

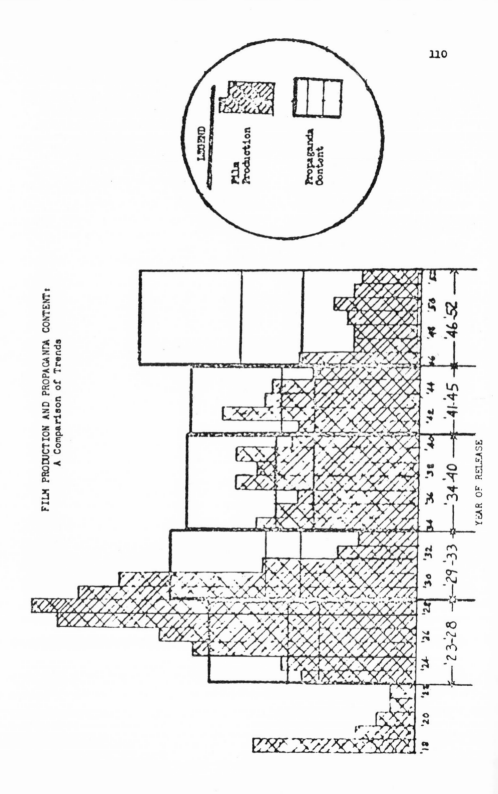

FILM PRODUCTION AND PROPAGANDA CONTENT:
A Comparison of Trends

Summary

The measurement of propaganda content described in this chapter, in conjunction with data on film production, shows that the role of the Communist Party in Soviet film affairs has not been so overpowering as to prevent some resistance on the part of film artists whenever the interests of the Party and the artists came into conflict. More than once, the Party's attempts to dominate the film industry came close to destroying that industry, insofar as film production dwindled dangerously close to zero. In 1933 and again in 1952 the party nearly terminated the production of feature films by means of political demands that threatened the heart of the artistic profession—the right to free and unlimited self-expression. Thus the power of the Party was circumscribed by the indispensability of the artist and his determination to resist political pressure. As a result of these events, both the Party and the artists developed a better understanding of the role of the Party, thus setting the stage for future compromises that would insure the revival of Soviet film production and the viability of the motion picture industry in the U.S.S.R.

CHAPTER VI

THE POWER OF THE ARTIST

The Arts as a Profession

The amateur artist has never found a place in the Soviet film
industry. The mainstay of the industry has been the professional
artist—be he a writer, director, cameraman, actor or designer. The
profession of Soviet artist is quite complicated in the motion-picture
industry; aside from a basic artistic inclination, the professional has
made his way on the strength of numerous talents and a basic core of
experience as a professional artist. Therefore, he is not developed
"overnight"—nor is he easily replaced by amateurs.

One type of film artist—the director—can serve as an illustration of the professionalization of the film artist. Although other
professional specialists differ from the directors in many respects,
they share certain characteristics which are typical of all professional
artists in the film industry, and these characteristics will be stressed
in the description of the director's professional life.

There are a number of prerequisites necessary to adequate performance of the role of film director in the Soviet Union today, and
these requirements are even more crucial to those whose performance of
the role goes beyond mere adequacy and reaches excellence. Prerequisites
are postulated both by the general responsibilities of the role itself

and by the administrators of the Communist Party and Soviet State. Proper interpretation of plans and decrees, for example, is an important prerequisite to adequate role performance for every film director. The successful production of films depends largely on the director's correct interpretation of his own role, but at the same time the officials of the Party and State specify other requirements on such matters as film content, participation in the training of new cadres, agitation for higher standards of popular film-art appreciation, and so on. It is necessary for the film director to elicit interpretations of higher-level decisions from the administrators with whom he deals, and simultaneously the director has to attempt his own interpretations of higher-level decisions because the interpretations of others may be at variance with the intent behind the actual decrees.

Not only is the director expected to interpret decrees accurately, but he is also expected to anticipate forthcoming plans and regulations to the best of his ability. The fact that a film usually takes between one and three years to produce means that shrewd guesses regarding future trends in Soviet policy are very much in order; bad guesses result in bad films, often in useless films. The director has to take risks and his reputation hangs in the balance.

Insofar as the film director coordinates the activities of many specialists, such as actors, camera-men, sound and lighting technicians, and editors, the total result of their combined efforts will be attributed to the director as much as to all of the others, and he is therefore placed in the position of assuming credit for their coordinated successes and taking blame for their individual failures. Similarly, the director may be held culpable if the original scenario contained "unacceptable" themes or scenes which were not eliminated prior to actual production of the film, due to carelessness or hesitancy on the part of reviewers. In both cases, the director becomes a figure-head for the entire production staff; it is his name more than any other which is associated with a film (although actors and actresses have become more prominent in this respect in recent years). Some personalities do not fare very well under this pressure, and it is evident that a "tough" personality structure is required of the Soviet film director because heavy responsibilities are inherent in his role.

The film director must be a capable administrator and coordinator. He cannot long afford to be unpopular among those who work with him in the production of films, nor can he lack any of the talents required for the simultaneous direction of activities of many people, many of them specialists in their own right. It is probably not necessary for the director to know everything about acting, lighting, photography, and so on, but it is absolutely indispensable that he work with many skilled persons in such a way as to bring into the film the combined results of all their knowledge and talents. This is not only a matter of administrative skill, but also of artistic judgment. The film director cannot perform his role adequately without considerable administrative and artistic talent.

Because films are generally shown to broad segments of the total Soviet population, the director must have far-flung interests. He must continuously educate himself about various phases of contemporary Soviet life and cannot shun actual study of many different occupational roles,

political problems, economic projects, and scientific developments.
He must be able to direct films which portray modern Soviet life in
terms of the prevailing style, "socialist realism." This requires in-
sight into the characteristics of popular, as opposed to esoteric,
film-art; the film medium in the U.S.S.R. demands directors of
"people's films." Innovation, pessimism, and other disreputable tendencies are taboo.

The ability to work under pressure is another important requirement.
The contemporary Soviet film director is always pressed for time, and
economy demands are no less severe. Maximum speed of film production
competes with low-cost production of films for the distinction of being
the most pressing requirement; both are always emphasized and can create intolerable working conditions for those who perform well only when
ample funds and time are available to them.

It is also necessary for directors to place the demands of film
critics ahead of popular sentiment in evaluating the general reaction
to films. The critic is closer to the administrators of the film industry and can exert pressure on directors much more readily and sig-
nificantly than can the Soviet film audience. Thus, persons who continuously ignore critics of the professional variety for the sake of
keeping more in line with actual popular preferences are eventually
bound to find themselves in trouble. To avoid chronic criticism, which
can lead to further complications, the director must be willing to adhere closely to the demands of the professional film critics, even when
they become more severe and caustic than popular sentiment would war-
rant. The director must adjust to the principle that his films are

intended primarily to educate the public and that he cannot therefore be limited by the dictates of popular demand; rather, he must give the public what the Communist Party wants, as directives are interpreted by the professional film critic who makes his reactions to films known through the press.

Film directors must not only be willing to accept criticism from reviewers, but they must criticize their own films publicly and must strain friendly relations with other personnel in the industry by criticizing their performance as well. The criticism is supposed to be constructive, of course, but the effect of frequent self-criticism and openly expressed mutual criticism among working associates has its unpleasant aspects. Some persons who could absorb much criticism from professional critics and continue to work effectively nevertheless might balk when required to indulge in abundant self-criticism and public disapprobation of close associates. Willingness to indulge frequently in this Soviet activity must be considered a prerequisite to a successful career as film director.

Although not all film directors are required to spend time in teaching their skills to others at the studios or training institutes, a number of the leading directors spend part or all of their time as instructors, and the ability to teach others may be considered a definite asset for optimum performance of the director's role. Similarly, the ability to discuss film-art appreciation at conferences and before Soviet audiences, while not absolutely necessary, will stand the director in good stead. There are frequent opportunities to speak at meetings of Film Society members, at film festivals, in movie theaters, and also in factory clubrooms, military establishments, and the like. Such personal contact with the vast film audience is appreciated by the officials of the Party and the film industry.

Many directors have received training at one or more of the many film studio schools. A smaller number have studied at the institutes which train directors and other film industry personnel. Although formal training in film-art was not expected of directors during the 1920's, it became increasingly important during the 1930's and the number of directors with formal film training is now quite impressive. Formal film training is now combined with ideological instruction. Although some study of "political grammar," dialectical materialism, and similar subjects is now common in most Soviet schools, only a small number of students receive advanced training in these subjects--but film directors are expected to have a firm grasp of the essential elements of Soviet ideology.

Research and writing abilities are rewarded. Although few directors publish books on film history and film theory, many write occasional articles for the film industry journal and for other Soviet publications. This activity is encouraged, partly to increase popular appreciation of film-art, partly to inform the Soviet population about the nature of artistic and intellectual activity, and partly to demonstrate the political consciousness and loyalty of Soviet intellectuals and artists.

Work in the realm of art that is hedged about with various regulations, requirements, and restrictions is not easy for an artist who likes to have a free hand in making decisions and planning his work.

Censorship, severe criticism and destruction of artistic works are also detrimental to creativity. Nevertheless, successful Soviet directors must be able to cope with recurring situations that contain many of these disturbing elements.

Another requirement for adequate role performance is the willingness to recant and to admit "errors" frequently. This "self-criticism" often means confession that the critics are correct. Together with self-criticism and confession there is supposed to be a promise to do better "next time." The public confession, which has become an integral part of the role of the Soviet film director, probably has a "therapeutic" value, but not everyone is likely to enter a profession where this sort of behavior is constantly required.

As regards membership in the Communistic Party, or the Komsomol, this has not become mandatory for professional film directors, but such memberships aided more than one director to launch a career. Moreover, Party members probably enjoy special privileges—but they also have extra responsibilities.

The Availability of Film Artists

The Communist Party has repeatedly complained about shortages of "talented" artists. This allegation has been echoed by some Westerners (such as Catherine de la Roche, a British film critic) who have observed developments in the Soviet motion picture industry. This criticism of professional film artists has been related not only to the quality of Soviet films but also to their quantity, on the grounds that unartistic films cannot be released because they do not satisfy the "high requirements of the Soviet audience" (read Communist Party).

Whatever truth may be contained in this official criticism, it cannot explain the great variations in Soviet film production unless it could also be demonstrated that the availability of talented artists varied in direct proportion to the marked increases and decreases in productivity. Thus the alleged shortage of talented artists must have occurred during the period of low productivity (the period 1929-1933 and the period 1946-1952)—if the allegation has any substance.

The Soviet motion picture industry was always in a position to attract scenario writers from the ranks of novelists and playwrights because of the high financial reward for working in the film industry; for the same reason, actors and actresses could readily be lured from the theater to the films. Therefore, the alleged shortage of professional artists in the motion picture industry most likely pertained to the professional motion picture directors, whose special talents and experience were described in the previous section of this chapter. Now it can be demonstrated that an abundant number of experienced film directors was available to the Soviet film industry administration at all times and that the number of "idle" (but experienced) professional film directors was greatest during the periods when film production was low. Thus, the alleged shortage of professional artists can only mean one of two things: either the professional artists temporarily ceased—voluntarily or involuntarily—to participate fully in film production, or else the Communist Party fabricated a weak excuse for the shortage of new films during the periods when production declined.

The Productivity of Soviet Film Directors

A compilation of work histories for more than 200 film directors employed in the Soviet motion picture industry lends itself to an analysis of the productivity of these directors. Thus, it is possible to ascertain (within a small margin of error) how many Soviet directors released only one film between 1918 and 1952, how many released two films, and so on. This measure of activity and experience is depicted graphically on the page that follows.

The greatest output was achieved by the director Yakov Protazanov, who released 19 Soviet films prior to his death in 1945. The directors Amo Bek-Nazarov and Vladimir Gardin each released 14 films between 1913 and 1952. More than a score of other directors released at least ten films each during the same period. Among these very active and experienced directors were Grigori Aleksandrov, Mikhail Chiaureli, Mark Donskoi, Friedrich Ermler, Aleksander Ivanovski, Lev Kuleshov, Ivan Perestiani, Vladimir Petrov, Vsevolod Pudovkin, Ivan Pyr'yev, Yuli Raizman, Abram Room, Grigori Roshal' and several others.

A group of 41 directors released an average of ten films each—that is, more than 400 films. During the same period, approximately 300 other films were released by 185 other directors. While this latter group of directors, who averaged less than two films per director, may be characterized as the "inexperienced" film directors of the Soviet Union, the 41 directors who released an average of ten films each may be characterized as the most active and experienced directors of the Soviet film industry. The active and experienced film directors each released <u>at least</u> six films between 1918 and 1952.

Activity of Soviet Feature Film Directors During the Period 1918 - 1952

ALL FEATURE FILM DIRECTORS*

53 % of all Directors released no more than one film,** accounting for...

29 % released 2 - 5 films, accounting for...

18 % released 6 or more films, accounting for...

...14 % of all Films

...28 % of all Films

...58 % of all Films

ALL FEATURE FILMS*

* A total of 706 films were released by 226 directors between 1918 and 1952, according to available data.

** Note: Whenever two directors collaborated on one film, each was credited one-half.

These statistics are on the conservative side. They do not account for all Soviet films, because complete information was not always available. Nevertheless, they present a fairly reliable picture of the productivity of Soviet film directors.

The Availability of Active and Experienced Directors

Study of the group of 41 active and experienced Soviet directors indicates that more than one-half of this group was available to the film industry administration at all times, despite attrition due to retirement, death and so on. Analysis of the period of active service for each director (beginning in each instance in the year when the director released his first independent production, and ending with the year in which his most recent film was released) shows that the Soviet film industry had at least 22 active and experienced directors on hand at all times—and these figures are conservative. The composition and availability of this group of 41 directors is depicted in a chart on the page that follows.

Some directors among this group came to the Soviet film industry from the pre-revolutionary Russian movie business, where most had been film directors before 1918. Among these were the directors Bek-Nazarov, Preobrazhenskaya, Chardynin, Kuleshov, Razumnyi, Protazanov, Perestiani, Sabinski, Gardin and Zhelyabushski. Some had reached middle-age by 1918, and retired after serving the Soviet film industry for a number of years.

Thus, while the Soviet film industry "inherited" some experienced directors, most of these had to be replaced rather quickly by younger

123

AVAILABILITY OF ACTIVE AND EXPERIENCED DIRECTORS

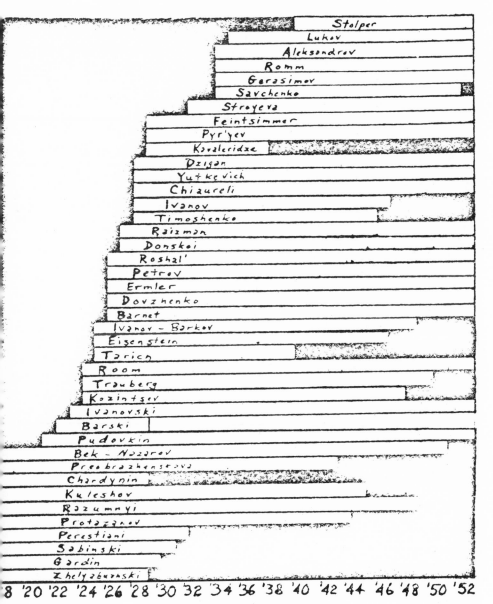

TIME PERIOD OF AVAILABILITY

From year when the director's first independent production was released.

124

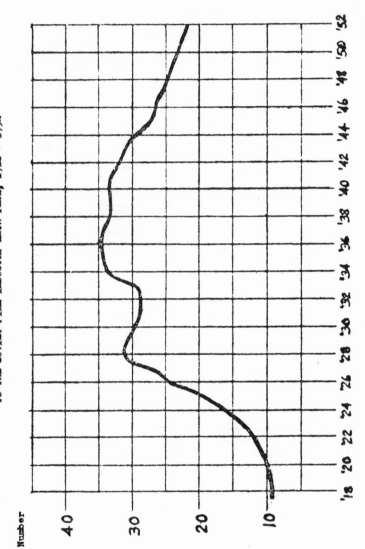

THE NUMBER OF ACTIVE AND EXPERIENCED FILM DIRECTORS AVAILABLE

TO THE SOVIET FILM INDUSTRY EACH YEAR, 1918 – 1952

Number

40

30

20

10

'18, '20, '22, '24, '26, '28, '30, '32, '34, '36, '38, '40, '42, '44, '46, '48, '50, '52

Year

Soviet directors. Furthermore, the ambitious plans of the Soviet film administration required a considerable expansion of the productive capacity of the film studios, and the need for more professional film directors was soon apparent. A decade after the 1917 Revolution, the Soviet film industry had available the services of 31 of the 41 persons who constituted the group of most active and experienced Soviet film directors.

After 1928, the number of directors in this group declined slightly because of retirement and death, but the group continued to number at least 25 persons even during the year 1933—when less than 10 new Soviet films were released. On the basis of these statistics, any "shortage" of talented film directors must be attributed to an inability to work on the part of some Soviet directors, rather than on a total lack of active and experienced men. In other words, the film directors were there, but the freedom to create may have been absent. This would confirm the thesis that film artists contributed to the decline in film production by making themselves "temporarily unavailable" until the Communist Party compromised by relieving the pressure it had brought to bear on the artists of the film industry.

When the availability of active and experienced film directors is compared with annual film production statistics (see next page), it seems apparent that an adequate—even abundant—number of experienced directors were always on hand, especially during the years when production dipped and fewer directors were actually engaged in film work. This is all the more apparent in view of the fact that more than 50 films were produced in 1928, when less than 35 active and experienced directors

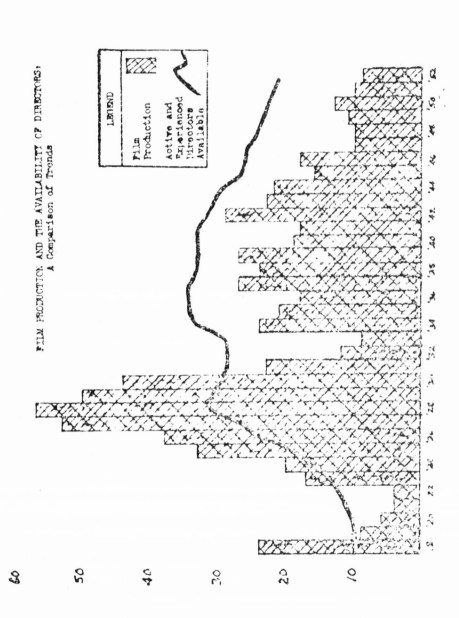

FILM PRODUCTION AND THE AVAILABILITY OF DIRECTORS:
A Comparison of Trends

were employed in the film industry; in 1928 the speed of film production was so great that several of the most active and experienced
directors released more than one film in the same year; in addition,
a number of the less experienced directors also released films that
year. During 1933, on the other hand, only nine films were released
although 27 active and experienced directors were available. Similarly
in 1952 only nine films were released although 21 active and experienced
directors were available.

It is interesting, too, that fewer directors were apparently available in 1952 than in 1933. This difference is partly spurious, because
the statistics are based on films released by each director between
1918 and 1952—thereby omitting some of the newcomers to the film industry who might have been rapidly becoming active and experienced, even
though they had not yet released six films by 1952. (Six films was the
arbitrary minimum used to distinguish between the experienced and the
inexperienced directors for purposes of this analysis.) Nevertheless,
there may be a genuine difference, due to the fact that newcomers were
actually being discouraged during the late 1940's because the main
directing assignments were going exclusively to the most active and most
experienced film directors. In the words of the Soviet film industry's
chief administrator, Ivan Bol'shakov, writing in the publication
Sovetskoye iskusstvo (Soviet Art) in March of 1951, ". . . the advance-
ment of young directors has been at a standstill for the past ten to
fifteen years."[1] This admission is all the more surprising because

---

[1]Sovetskoye iskusstvo, March 20, 1951; translated in Current Digest
of the Soviet Press, Volume III, Number 17, pp. 7-10.

Bol'shakov's deputy, Pereslavtsev, was going to great lengths to justify

the policy of favoring the more experienced directors with feature film

directing assignments:

> Excessive haste in promoting young directors right from the school-
> bench to independent professional work is . . . fraught with a cer-
> tain element of risk, not merely because it can lead to waste of
> tremendous state funds, but even more because a failure . . . leads
> not merely to distrust of those who failed . . . but to distrust
> of young directors in general. . . . There is another reason why
> young film directors are . . . promoted slowly. The reason is that
> the Soviet film industry has available a large [sic] number of
> so-called "old" (that is, established) directors, most of whom are
> outstanding professional masters of film work, and it is natural
> that assignments to produce films should go to them first of all.[2]

Meanwhile, however, Bol'shakov's other deputy, Shcherbina, was complain-

ing in Pravda that "many great directors, known for their excellent films,

have not participated in film production for several years."[3] It is well

worth noting that Comrade Shcherbina did not say "a few" or "some"; he

said "many"!

Soviet film directors were well aware of the situation. The promi-

nent director Ivan Pyr'yev, one of the group of 41 most active and ex-

perienced directors, wrote an article entitled "Where a Creative Atmos-

phere is Lacking . . ." which was published in 1952; he said: "Our art

was ossified. Filming assignments went only to the most trusted direc-

tors. . . . The road was barred to youth. During the last five years

no new names have appeared in our art . . ."[4]

---

[2]Pereslavtsev, V., "On Young Professional Cadres of the Soviet Cinema," Literaturnaya gazeta, November 24, 1951, pp. 2-4.

[3]Pravda, July 10, 1948.

[4]Pyr'yev, Ivan, "Tam gde net tvorcheskoe atmosfery," Literaturnaya gazeta, September 2, 1952.

It was not until after Stalin's death, however, that the deleterious consequences of the post-war policies in the film industry were aired. Finally, on July 1, 1954, the newspaper <u>Literaturnaya gazeta</u>, organ of the Union of Professional Writers, admitted in print what had been going on:

> We have distinguished film directors . . . artists with world-wide reputations. But it has come to the point where they do very little work. For four years I. Pyr'yev, M. Donskoi and A. Stolper have not been heard from. For five years A. Dovzhenko has not released a single new film. Seven years have passed since L. Arnshtam produced his last film, and eight since the last one by F. Ermler . . .
>
> A large part of the blame falls on the top cinema officials. In planning film production, they have not taken into account the interests and the individual artistic bent of the director. And how is it possible to disregard the creative aspirations of the artist? For the prolonged silence of our leading directors the system itself is chiefly to blame . . .

---

[5]"Preodolet' nedostatki kinematografii" (Shortcomings in the Film Industry Must Be Overcome), <u>Literaturnaya gazeta</u>, Moscow, July 1, 1954.

CHAPTER VII

THE POWER OF THE AUDIENCE

Film audiences in the U.S.S.R. constitute the chief target for the ideological messages contained in Soviet films, but the Soviet audience also finances the film industry in the U.S.S.R. Therefore, the size and composition of the audience is of considerable importance to this analysis of the film industry, because the potential power of the audience is thereby made clear. An analysis of audience preferences (with respect to films) illustrates how this power is used.

The Size of the Film Audience

Estimates Based on Official Sources

Attempts to determine the actual size have been hindered somewhat by inconsistent data, but the magnitude and trend is clear. Evidently, the size of the film audience increased substantially for two decades, until more than one billion movie admissions were being sold annually in the U.S.S.R. by 1940. Although attendance declined during the Second World War, it undoubtedly increased again in the post-war period. The diminution in audience size was very substantial during World War II because of territorial and population losses, fluctuating morale, physical destruction of exhibition facilities, military requirements, and the difficulties of wartime life—and some of these factors also impeded post-war recovery. It is probable, however, that the size of the movie audience in 1952 again surpassed one billion admissions annually.

Several sets of published statistics, all based on Soviet data, are compared below:

Year	Set A*	Set B**	Set C†
1927	260,000,000		260,000,000
1928	240,000,000	310,000,000	240,000,000
1932	637,000,000		637,000,000
1934	442,000,000	440,000,000	
1935	545,000,000		
1936	708,000,000		650,000,000
1937	736,000,000		
1938	935,000,000	872,000,000	
1939		1,200,000,000	
1940			1,200,000,000
1941			900,000,000
1944			600,000,000
1945		573,000,000	

* New York Times, September 21, 1941, Section IX, p. 4.

** Inkeles, A., Public Opinion in Soviet Russia, 1950, p. 306.

† Composite of several other sources published outside the U.S.S.R. See Soviet Union Review, November 1928, pp. 172-73; "Fifteen Years of the Soviet Cinema," Economic Review of the Soviet Union, January 1935, p. 8; Verlinsky, V., "Motion Picture Industry in the Soviet Union," Journal of the Society of Motion Picture Engineers, January 1935, pp. 12, 15; Dickinson, T., and A. Lawson, "The Film in USSR--1937," Cine-Technician, August/September 1937, pp. 105-06; Manvell, R., Film, 1950, p. 187.

It should be mentioned that the <u>actual</u> increases in audience size did not keep pace with the <u>planned</u> increases which were called for in the vast economic programs promulgated in the U.S.S.R. to develop the national economy. According to available estimates, the actual size of the film audience during the final year (1932) of the first Five-Year-Plan era was only 25 to 50 percent of the planned target for movie attendance. There is reason to believe that the planned targets of later Five-Year-Plans were more realistic and were, consequently, fulfilled to a greater extent.

In any event, the government of the U.S.S.R. derived considerable financial income from the money spent by audiences at the box-office, regardless of planned targets. Financial data covering four successive years suggest both the magnitude and the increase in revenue collected by the government of the U.S.S.R. from the domestic film audience.[1]

Year	Revenue (in Rubles)
1931	58,500,000
1932	240,000,000
1933	285,000,000
1934	529,000,000

In conclusion, the data bear out the contention that the movie audience in the U.S.S.R. increased considerably between the 1920's and 1940. The decline in audience size during the second World War and the early post-war years is evidenced by statistics on movie theater destruction and losses of movie projection equipment, in addition to estimates

[1]Kotiev, B., "Popularization of the Cinema in the U.S.S.R.," in <u>Soviet Cinema</u>, edited by A. Arosev, Moscow, VOKS, 1935, p. 215.

of the audience size--but data for the early 1950's indicate a recovery
to the level of 1939-1940, the best pre-war years.

Estimates Based on Interviews with Soviet Citizens

About ten years ago, some information about movie attendance
habits was obtained from former citizens of the U.S.S.R. By means of
personal interviews and self-administered questionnaires which focused
on their life-experiences in the Soviet Union, estimates of their own
former movie attendance habits were obtained from several thousand respondents. The data were obtained during the year 1950 by social scientists of the Russian Research Center at Harvard University.

The estimates of their own movie attendance obtained from former
citizens of the U.S.S.R. were either qualitative or quantitative, depending on the form of the question posed in the Harvard survey. About
2,500 persons provided a qualitative estimate by answering a check-list
question phrased as follows: "While you were in the Soviet Union, how
often did you go to the movies?" Three alternative answers were suggested in the questionnaire: "Frequently," "Seldom," "Never."

A second kind of estimate, which was more quantitative, was obtained
from approximately 250 respondents by means of personal interviews. Respondents were generally asked this question: "How often did you attend
the movies during a typical month in the year 1940?" (The year 1940 was
chosen as the most recent peace-time year during which most of the respondents had lived in the U.S.S.R.) Interviewers occasionally varied
the form of the question, especially with reference to the year, so as
to obtain more recent information from post-war residents of the U.S.S.R.

About nine-tenths of the estimates made about film attendance pertained to the year 1940, however, because only one-tenth of those interviewed had lived in the Soviet Union after the Second World War.

Comparison of qualitative and quantitative estimates was facilitated by obtaining both kinds of estimates from approximately 40 respondents. This comparison not only revealed a high degree of consistency in the answers, but also made possible the development of standards for analysis of the entire body of data. Nearly 2500 individuals made qualitative estimates of their frequency of movie attendance (in the U.S.S.R.) as follows:

Percentage				Number of Respondents
"Frequently"	"Seldom"	"Never"	Total	
36.5%	52%	11.5%	100%	(2465)

Interviewers obtained some quantitative information from nearly 250 respondents asked to estimate their frequency of movie attendance in the U.S.S.R. during a typical month in the year 1940, as follows:

Percentage					Number of Respondents
At least 4 times per month	1 to 3 times per month	Less than once per month	Never	Total	
36%	38%	20%	6%	100%	(244)

For this group the average monthly movie attendance could be expressed as 3.5 times per month (the mean), 2.3 times per month (the median), or 4.0 times per month (the mode).[2]

---

[2]It is interesting to compare these figures with data on attendance frequencies among movie-goers in other countries. The proportions and averages are not very different from comparable European or American

While these figures cannot be projected to the Soviet population with much reliability, they suggest that the magnitude of the official Soviet attendance figures for 1940 is quite reasonable as an estimate of the size of the domestic audience for films in the U.S.S.R.

The Composition of the Film Audience

Not all Soviet citizens go to the movies to the same extent. Analysis of the questionnaires obtained by Harvard University's Russian Research Center shows that three factors are highly correlated with frequent attendance. These factors are the availability of motion picture performances, the resources of the individual, and the style-of-life of those social groups with which the individual coordinates his own activities.

The availability of motion-picture performances varies with residence. In general, city dwellers have greater access to movies than town residents, but the latter find films more readily available than do rural inhabitants.

Resources of the individual which influence movie attendance frequencies include money and leisure-time.

With regard to style-of-life, various social groups in the U.S.S.R. had developed characteristic patterns of movie attendance by 1940. Differences are greatest between various age groups, and various occupational groups.

statistics. See for example, the survey results for several countries and several time periods which are reported in Public Opinion, 1935-1946, edited by Hadley Cantril, Princeton, Princeton University Press, 1951, pp. 485-90.

The statistical data based on the questionnaires obtained by the Russian Research Center are expressed (on the pages that follow) so as to focus attention on the four significant figures relating to any given group of respondents:

1. The percentage of respondents who stated that they attended the movies "frequently."

2. The percentage who stated that they attended "seldom."

3. The percentage who indicated that they "never" attended movies.

4. The number of respondents comprising the group.

Thus, the total sample of respondents may be summarized as follows:

Percentage				Number of Respondents
"Frequently"	"Seldom"	"Never"	Total	
36.5	52	11.5	100	(2465)

Those few who failed to answer the question on movie attendance are omitted from all the tabulations.

Availability of Performances

The differences in availability of movies in cities, towns, and villages of the U.S.S.R. is evident from data on the distribution of film exhibition facilities, but is also reflected in answers obtained from the sample of respondents. The results follow:

	Percentage				Number of Respondents
	"Frequently"	"Seldom"	"Never"	Total	
City residents	50	46	04	100	(1153)
Town residents	36	57	07	100	(661)
Rural residents	12	56	32	100	(568)

These statistics support the hypothesis that availability is a determinant of attendance, but they also reflect other differences: different styles-of-life for certain age and social groups, and differences in financial resources. The differences between city, town and village persist, however, even when age and educational attainment (a basis for distinguishing between social groups) is held constant. Thus, analysis of city-town-rural differences among groups of respondents roughly equivalent in age and formal education indicated fairly consistent trends in the predicated direction—that is, differences between city, town and village were still present.

Further evidence that the differential availability of movie theaters in cities, towns and rural areas affected frequency of movie attendance was derived from statistics for specific occupational groups:

Occupation		Percentage				Number of Respondents
		Frequently	Seldom	Never	Total	
Applied Sciences and Professions	City	44	53	03	100	(197)
	Town	35	62	03	100	(40)
	Rural	22	67	11	100	(9)
Semi-professional occupations	City	53	44	03	100	(116)
	Town	39	61	00	100	(61)
	Rural	27	70	03	100	(30)
"White Collar" occupations	City	49	49	02	100	(186)
	Town	44	55	01	100	(98)
	Rural	30	67	03	100	(30)
Skilled and semi-skilled occupations	City	37	57	06	100	(191)
	Town	32	59	09	100	(188)
	Rural	13	57	30	100	(105)
Unskilled occupations	City	13	80	07	100	(30)
	Town	13	69	18	100	(45)
	Rural	11	67	22	100	(36)

Individual Resources

Resources of the individual which affect frequency of movie attendance to a significant degree include *time* and *money*. With respect to time, the greatest significance obtains for <u>total leisure time</u> available to the individual. Hours spent at work, and for travel to and from work, are negatively correlated with frequency of movie attendance, as may be seen in these statistics:

Daily Travel Time	Daily Work Time	Percentage				Number of Respondents
		Frequently	Seldom	Never	Total	
Less than one hour	Less than nine hours	52	45	03	100	(268)
	Nine hours or more	41	53	06	100	(159)
One hour or more	Less than nine hours	40	56	04	100	(580)
	Nine hours or more	30	60	10	100	(458)

Personal <u>resources</u> which affected frequency of movie attendance include not only time, but also money. In the absence of income data, however, precise information about personal financial resources was not available.

Style of Life

One of the most widely recognized characteristics of movie-goers is their low age. This factor is quite apparent in the total sample:

Age in 1940	Percentage				Number of Respondents
	Frequently	Seldom	Never	Total	
Under 10	40	56	04	100	(25)
11 – 15	48	47	05	100	(168)
16 – 20	47	44	09	100	(22)
21 – 25	50	39	11	100	(363)
26 – 30	41	51	08	100	(307)
31 – 35	34	54	12	100	(256)
36 – 40	26	62	12	100	(278)
41 – 45	21	64	15	100	(230)
46 – 50	18	61	21	100	(126)
Over 50	23	58	19	100	(124)

World War II seriously disrupted conventional movie attendance patterns; in addition, most of the respondents left the U.S.S.R. between 1940 and 1950. Therefore, respondents' ages around 1940 are actually of greater significance than the respondents' ages at the time of the interview (1950).

The analysis of movie attendance by various occupational groups reveals another dimension of the style of life and its relation to film-going. The "middle class" occupations are characterized by a high frequency of attendance, compared to the "lower class" occupations. The "upper class" occupations also report more frequent attendance than the "lower class" occupations. (See statistics at the top of the following page.) As previously indicated, these trends are maintained when residence (city, town, village) is held constant.

| | Percentage | | | | Number of Respondents |
	Frequently	Seldom	Never	Total	
Managers and Military	65	35	00	100	(57)
Arts	63	37	00	100	(76)
Applied sciences	40	60	00	100	(109)
Professions	41	56	03	100	(146)
Semi-professionals	45	54	01	100	(208)
"White-collar"	45	53	02	100	(320)
Skilled workers	33	59	08	100	(166)
Semi-skilled workers	29	56	15	100	(333)
Unskilled workers	12	70	18	100	(113)
Collective farmers	06	48	46	100	(269)
Housewives	33	52	15	100	(58)
Advanced students	66	33	01	100	(186)
Elementary students	47	50	03	100	(195)

A similar "style of life" trend is revealed by an analysis of military rank among those respondents who served in the armed forces:

| | Percentage | | | | Number of Respondents |
	Frequently	Seldom	Never	Total	
Commissioned officers	62	37	01	100	(215)
Non-commissioned officers	53	41	06	100	(103)
Enlisted men	29	60	11	100	(239)

Note also the difference between farming and other rural occupations:

Collective farmers	06	48	46	100	(269)
All other rural occupations	13	69	18	100	(61)

In conclusion, this analysis of the composition of Soviet film audiences indicates that they are not composed exclusively of illiterate

peasants or workers who might be pleased to see any kind of film whatso-
ever. Rather, this analysis suggests that the typical Soviet film audience is likely to include a considerable proportion of "middle class"
citizens employed in white-collar or semi-professional occupations.
Further, the audiences are likely to be youthful, but not immature. On
this basis, it is possible to conceive of an audience for Soviet films
that is somewhat discriminating in its tastes and alert to the differences in the content of various films exhibited in the Soviet Union.
Thus, the predominantly urban character of the audience becomes an important consideration, because urban dwellers are in the best position
to learn about film content (from others who have seen the picture) before deciding whether or not to go to see any particular film. This
informal source of information about motion pictures is very important,
as it empowers many potential film-goers to express their preferences
for one or another type of film content merely by deciding in each instance
whether "to go or not to go" to see a particular film.

The Film Preferences of Soviet Audiences

Preferences with respect to motion pictures can vary not only from
person to person, but also from time to time and from mood to mood.
Furthermore, some people have more distinct preferences than others. In
addition, a film can satisfy preferences to varying degrees. Thus it is
meaningful to speak of degrees of satisfaction.

It must be pointed out, too, that film audiences, like Party officials and film artists, are continually forced to make compromises. The
Soviet citizen is generally free to attend or not to attend, but his

choice of films is necessarily limited if he decides to go to the movies. Therefore, the preferences of Soviet audiences--as measured by box office figures--lend themselves to more than one interpretation, particularly because a film must be judged as a unit by the spectator as he decides whether or not he will see it.

Film audiences, nevertheless, react to more than one aspect of a motion picture. Analysis of comments made about films (See Chapter 4) indicates some of the aspects that concern film audiences. Audiences tend to classify films into certain types: adventure films, comedies, satires, melodramas, and so on. Films are also classified by themes: patriotism, productivity, progress, and so on. Audiences also react to the tempo of the action, the dialogue and the change of scenes; they comment on the technical aspects of the film, such as the photography, the sound, or the color. Sometimes they discuss the casting and the acting. Most people will react, too, to the general topic of the film, be it life on a collective farm or the biography of a Tsarist general; in this connection, the treatment of the topic will also elicit comments to the effect that the plot is too complicated, or the hero is too idealized, or the villains are too stereotyped, etc. (If the treatment satisfies the audience, detailed criticisms are replaced by generalized statements of praise; "the film was good," or "it was enjoyable," or "it was nice.") Thus, the audience reacts to some or all of these elements in every film, and the final evaluation may be based on a composite judgment, not merely one specific feature.

Because a forced optimism in films is consistently demanded by the Communist Party in its directives to film makers, Soviet audiences react

in particular to this official style which is called "socialist realism."
Sometimes the reaction to the official style is differentiated further
into two components: "truthfulness" and "politicization." Thus, a film
may be considered "true," but "too political"; it may be considered both
"untrue" and "too political." Sometimes a film is even considered
"politically necessary" although it is not "truthful"--a view of films
that defines them chiefly as a medium for socially useful propaganda.
(This comes very close to being the "official view" endorsed by the Communist Party, but it is also accepted by some Soviet citizens.) It
should be noted, however, that changes in the "Party line" have frequently
altered the official definition of what is true and what is not, so that
the Soviet film may portray "reality" in different ways at different
times. To the extent that the Soviet citizen is persuaded to change his
own view of reality as well, he may react in identical fashion to different films (on the same subject) at different times.

Some Soviet citizens suspect film makers of a manipulative intent--
either in general, or in particular pictures--and this suspicion may
affect the credibility of the film and the satisfaction derived from
seeing it. Other people claim to have developed an "immunity" to official propaganda which enables them to enjoy the non-political content
while dismissing the propaganda as "silly" or "unimportant." Still others
continually attempt to measure the degree of truthfulness in films; they
look for details which can be confirmed or disproved by their own experi-
ences--partly to test the dependability of Party-approved films (as well
as other mass communications), and partly to glean useful information
from films. This "reality testing" is not always ossible--particularly

with respect to films with historical or foreign settings, but their
very inability to "disprove" these films makes them more enjoyable for
some members of the Soviet film audience.

Some persons approach the matter of "truthfulness" in films from
another standpoint: they assert that "artistic truth" should not be
equated with literal truth and that fantasy needs no justification. In
this view, it is possible to improve on the "truth" for the sake of
dramatic effect, and it is perfectly reasonable to enjoy every particle
of the national mythology either as entertainment or as ritual. Thus
there are some who do not expect films to be literally realistic or
literally truthful, and some of these persons like all Soviet films.

Expression of Audience Preferences

The point has been made throughout this thesis that Soviet audiences
express their preferences and demonstrate their power at the box office.
While this is the most convincing and thorough expression of audience
reaction to films, there are numerous other ways in which Soviet audiences can and do evaluate motion pictures. Some of these ways are poten-
tially very useful to film makers and the Party, because audiences have
the opportunity to evaluate films before the pictures are released for
general exhibition. Thus, it is sometimes possible to anticipate box
office results, and to accommodate audience preferences before it is "too
late."

One of the earliest methods used to ascertain audience reaction was
the preview. Completed films were shown to a few workers' clubs, or to
a branch of the organization called the Society of Friends of the Soviet
Film—a group organized in the 1920's to encourage interest in film

production and appreciation. Sometimes previews were also arranged in rural areas. These previews were always followed by a general discussion to ascertain audience reaction.

There were also some attempts, particularly during the 1920's, to measure audience preferences in a systematic way. In 1928, for example, a group of 800 school children in Moscow filled out questionnaires intended to ascertain their reactions to films.[3] The Film Institute in Moscow had a Scientific Research Department which undertook such investigations from time to time.

Another method for eliciting audience reaction in some detail involved the mail. Soviet citizens were encouraged to write (signed or unsigned) letters to newspapers, or to film studios, so that their views could be made known. Occasionally such letters were published in the press, but more frequently they were sent to the studio administration offices for detailed study. Thus the motion picture industry learned more about audience preferences—to the extent that people were willing to write such letters.

One other method frequently used to elicit audience reaction was the Soviet equivalent of the suggestion box. Sometimes this took the form of a large notebook in which the audience could write comments about films; these books were usually located in the theater lobby near the exits. Occasionally a large blackboard was available instead. Both compliments and criticism were encouraged in this way.

_____

[3]Harper, S., Civic Training in Soviet Russia, 1929, p. 334.

To summarize, the Soviet film industry was able to learn something about audience preferences in various ways. While these methods did not measure a highly accurate cross section of public opinion, they did give some indication of audience sentiment—ahead of, and in greater detail than box office results.

Impressionistic Descriptions of Audience Preferences

Although no systematic accounts of audience preferences in the Soviet Union have been published to date, there are many impressionistic descriptions in print. Some of these refer to specific films and cannot be interpreted without a detailed consideration of the subject film, but others are of a more general nature and purport to give a comprehensive view of audience preferences. While the scientific value of these impressionistic descriptions is dubious, a few samples will be cited here by way of example:

A British journalist noted in 1928 that "ordinary American 'escape' films were much in demand in Moscow."[4]

A British drama critic, writing in the 1920's, observed that films based on folk-tales were "very popular with the Russian masses."[5]

According to a New York Times correspondent writing in 1926, American films were extremely popular in the Soviet Union. "Unable to afford to import enough American films to supply the demand, Soviet studios turned out imitation 'Amerikansky' pictures, with 'American' lighting, camera tricks, and fast action. Charlie Chaplin and Mary Pickford had their

---

[4]Simpson, C., "Films in Moscow," The Spectator, July 28, 1928, Number 141, p. 124.

[5]Carter, H., New Spirit in the Russian Theatre, London, 1929, p. 289.

Russian incarnations. Bolshevik Buster Keatons were chased by OGPU--
Keystone Cops around the Red Square."[6]

An American professor of political science concluded that the
"motion picture public clearly prefers the comic, picturesque, and ad-
venturous pictures produced abroad, but the peasants have no choice,
and go to the . . . show if they have the price of admission when it
happens to come their way."[7]

Another American political scientist, writing around 1936, noted
that "long before the factory worker lost interest in the 'battle of
the tractors,' the intellectuals were sick and tired of the moving pictures on this subject."[8]

The same American professor also noted that "after the colossal
strain of the first Five-Year-Plan, Mickey Mouse invaded the Soviet
Union, cinema directors got busy in pursuit of proletarian comedies and
more candid concessions were made to surviving desires . . ."[9]

A left-wing British writer observed in 1936 that ". . . all films
are popular. A vast public, much of it still in the early stages of
movie fascination, is hungry for films, and there are nowhere near enough
efficient craftsmen to produce them. A failure in our sense of the word
does not exist, alternative programmes being so few that almost every
film made is seen by every cinema-goer."[10]

---

[6] New York Times, November 7, 1926.

[7] Harper, S., Civic Training in Soviet Russia, 1929, p. 334.

[8] Lasswell, H., "Scope of Research on Propaganda and Dictatorship,"
in Propaganda and Dictatorship, edited by H. Childs, Princeton, Princeton
University Press, 1936, p. 108.

[9] Ibid., p. 111.

[10] Belfrage, C., "Russia's 'Gollywood,'" World Film News, September
1936, p. 16.

Another New York Times correspondent, writing in 1937, ventured the opinion that "the interest in classical films is far from satisfied by domestic productions, but few are imported . . ."[11]

During World War II, a publication of the U.S. Department of Commerce quoted a consular official to the effect that "Soviet audiences will look at anything, but seem to prefer foreign films of an entertainment nature."[12]

Another New York Times correspondent reported in 1947 that Soviet audiences were fond of films which have the stage, ballet, or opera for a background and include musical numbers. He added that "the masses also like war movies, but the intelligentsia prefer film biographies of popular figures like Ivan the Terrible."[13]

A Soviet film director was quoted in an American wire service dispatch as having said that "some writers and directors think love is old-fashioned and that we should put attention on machines, tractors, and factories and forget life. We had a big fight . . . But the audiences objected. They wrote letters to the newspapers and . . . to officials protesting . . . that they wanted pictures with love and real life."[14]

An American journalist reported that "huge crowds start to queue up whenever there is a prospect of seeing a film made somewhere outside the Iron Curtain. . . . Many Russians tell me with a great air of superiority that the 'Tarzan' pictures are only for children or are nyekulturni, but

---

[11]New York Times, February 21, 1937, Section X, p. 4.

[12]Golden, N., Motion Picture Markets - 1944, Washington, U. S. Department of Commerce, p. 68.

[13]Middleton, D., "The Party Line Guides Russia's Movies," New York Times, July 27, 1947, Section VI, p. 13.

[14]New York Times, March 28, 1954, p. 1.

the reason that they speak with such authority is that just about
every Russian who has had the opportunity has gone to see the so-called
nyekulturni 'Tarzan' films."[15]

To summarize, these impressionistic generalizations are clearly of
limited value to social scientists accustomed to more refined first-hand
data, but they nevertheless convey the impression that Soviet citizens
will go to see any movie once—but they won't go to see it twice unless
they like it, and they probably won't like it if it isn't entertaining!
In addition, it is said that the best entertainment comes from abroad—
and that Soviet films achieve popularity by depicting folk tales, art,
music and romance.

Recall: Empirical Analysis of Audience Preferences

Although no comprehensive survey results are available, it is nevertheless possible to arrive at an estimate of audiences preferences on
the basis of an impartial, objective, empirical analysis of the data obtained in interviews conducted by a team of social scientists connected
with Harvard University. The body of data collected in approximately 250
personal interviews contains information not only about the frequency of
movie attendance in the Soviet Union, but also about audience preferences.
The most suitable type of information for purposes of this analysis is
the list of Soviet films named by former citizens of the U.S.S.R. in
response to the question: "Which films do you recall having seen in the
Soviet Union?"

---

[15]Higgins, M., Red Plush and Black Bread, New York, Doubleday, 1955,
pp. 183-184.

The "recall method" of measuring audience preference is not without
limitations, but a judicious use of the data can lead to fairly reliable
conclusions. While it cannot be assumed that recall is precisely equivalent to preference, this research technique has frequently been used as
a means for estimating preference. In this connection, it should be
noted that respondents were interviewed in the year 1950 about films
they had seen during the period prior to 1941; therefore, it may be
assumed that the films named by the respondents made a deep impression.
This impression was not always favorable, of course, but analysis of comments made by respondents when speaking of Soviet films indicates that
nearly all of the films mentioned were well liked by the respondents.
(This observation is supported by the generally accepted hypothesis that
pleasant memories are retained longer than unpleasant ones.) Thus an
analysis of the films named (or described) provides a basis for estimating the preference of these respondents, who were by no means uniformly
hostile to Soviet films (see Chapter 4).

About 125 films were recalled by respondents. The overwhelming
majority of these films had been released by Soviet studios during the
1930's. Some titles were mentioned more frequently than others, of
course; the film "Chapayev" (1934) was mentioned by one out of every
seven respondents, and the film "Peter the Great" (1937) was named by
one out of every ten. Two other pictures frequently mentioned were
"Alexander Nevski" (1938) and "Lenin in October" (1937). Altogether
there were about 350 mentions of approximately 125 Soviet films.

The Soviet films mentioned by respondents were analyzed to measure
their propaganda content, giving the proper weight to the frequency of

mentions. (The measurement technique—which rated propaganda content
in terms of time period, political affiliation of the hero, problem and
solution—has already been described in Chapter 5.) A composite measure
of the propaganda content in the films mentioned by the respondents was
computed on the basis of the ratings. Thus, an estimate of the propaganda content of these films was obtained.

To ascertain whether Soviet audiences were satisfied or dissatisfied
with the degree of propaganda content in Soviet films, the group of
motion pictures mentioned (and presumably preferred) by the respondents
was compared with all Soviet films produced between 1934 and 1940 in
terms of propaganda content. The comparison is depicted in the chart
on the page that follows. There is virtually no difference, apparently,
between the two groups of films—those recalled by respondents, and those
produced by Soviet studios—with regard to the composite measure of
propaganda content. Thus it seems reasonable to conclude that the average Soviet film-goer was generally satisfied with the film fare produced
in Soviet studios during the period 1934-1940. It cannot be concluded,
however, that Soviet film audiences were satisfied with each and every
Soviet film during that period; nor can it be assumed that Soviet film
audiences were equally satisfied with films produced during other periods,
particularly the periods 1929-1933 and 1946-1952 when the level of propaganda content was somewhat higher than during the period 1934-1940.

Since the group of respondents consisted of persons who left the
Soviet Union and resisted efforts to make them return after the war, it
is reasonable to assume that they were not more favorably disposed to the
Communist regime than other Soviet citizens. Therefore the degree of

TIME PERIODS, POLITICAL AFFILIATION OF HEROES, PROBLEMS AND SOLUTIONS:
A Composite Measure of Propaganda Content

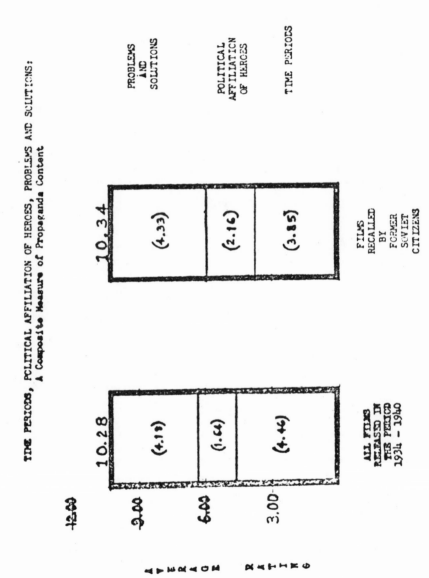

PROBLEMS
AND
SOLUTIONS

POLITICAL
AFFILIATION
OF HEROES

TIME PERIODS

10.34

(4.33)

(2.16)

(3.85)

FILMS
RECALLED
BY
FORMER
SOVIET
CITIZENS

10.28

(4.18)

(1.64)

(4.46)

ALL FILMS
RELEASED IN
THE PERIOD
1934 - 1940

12.00

9.00

6.00

3.00

AVERAGE RATING

satisfaction with Soviet film content expressed by these respondents can hardly be greater than the satisfaction which could be expected of the average Soviet film-goer. On the other hand, the conclusion can apply only to those who choose to see Soviet films; it does not apply to the entire Soviet population, which includes a substantial number of persons who seldom or never see Soviet films. This is why the present chapter has considered only the role of that part of the Soviet population which constitutes the audience for Soviet films.

PART IV

FILM PRODUCTION AND FILM CONTENT:
CONFLICT AND COMPROMISE

CHAPTER VIII

COMPROMISES ABOUT FILM CONTENT

The process of film production invariably consisted of many steps
and required from several months to several years. At each step, from
the initial plans to the final preview, it was possible to revise the
motion picture in some small detail or on a large scale. Although the
cost of changes was considerable (and sometimes exceeded that of the
original production) the practice of making continual changes was very
common. In some instances, films were even withdrawn from circulation
and returned to the studios to make additional changes.

In general, persons concerned with film production attempted to
anticipate the reaction of both those individuals who were authorized
to demand changes, and the film audiences who were expected to see the
film. Intuition played an important role in this process of anticipa-
tion, as did experience. It was generally understood that the film
producers had to be thoroughly familiar with the subject matter of the
film and also with audience preferences. Because of political pressures,
however, it was also of paramount importance that film producers be
thoroughly familiar with the long-range aims and current policies of the
political leadership. As political changes occurred frequently, it was
inevitable that film content would require continual adjustment. Another
consequence of these changes, however, was the tendency to avoid contemporary subject matter--but this tendency was frequently opposed by the

political leaders who wanted to use the film as a supplement to the press and radio as a means of up-to-date propaganda.

The conflict about contemporary subject matter was only one of many that required compromise. These compromises usually occurred at every step of the production process. Representatives of the Communist Party's point of view participated in the frequent conferences about the content of any specific film, as did the film artists—particularly the scenario writers and directors. On some occasions the future audience was represented: persons unconnected with the film industry were sometimes invited to discuss scenarios under consideration (and some scenarios were even published before actual production began); completed films were occasionally exhibited to "typical" audiences to obtain the spectators' reaction. Now and then, attempts were made to conduct audience surveys for the purpose of measuring the popularity of a film in advance of its general release, but this practice was infrequent. Spectators were also given the opportunity to write comments about films in a book available to them in the lobby of the movie theater, and these comments, together with others that came in the mail, were available to studio executives and other connected with the production of films.

Most newspapers and magazines assigned staff members to write reviews of newly released motion pictures, and the reviews not only discussed the film but also other movie reviews previously published elsewhere. These reviewers, like everyone else, attempted to consider both the wishes of the Communist Party and the preferences of the film audience. The more authoritative publications (such as the official newspapers of the army, government, and the party) tended to give primary

importance to the official "line," but reviews in other publications--
more remote from the centralized political authority--had to rely more
on the personal judgment of the critic and his circle of acquaintances.
The more specialized publications (such as newspapers and magazines for
farmers, miners, railroad men and so on) went even further in attempting
to relate the film reviews to the interests and preferences of their
readers, which meant that these film reviews gave some consideration to
the film audiences. Most of this published material came to the attention of the people connected with film studios, thus giving them a more
detailed reaction to a particular film than would have been possible on
the basis of box office figures alone. These opinions undoubtedly came
up for discussion at the frequent conferences that took place in the
movie studios between producers and representatives of the political
leadership. In this way, the audiences' point-of-view was considered in
discussions of film content, together with the all-important attendance
statistics.

Compromises During the Production Process

It is difficult to describe the details of changes in scenario and
film during the production period, for several reasons. First, few
people witnessed the conferences where decisions are made--especially at
the higher levels. Second, those in authority did not make it a practice
to publish the reasons for their decisions (although a few documents
are available and throw some light on the considerations involved).
Third, it would be difficult to analyze any decision-making process which
includes not only rational aspects but also esthetic considerations and

emotional appeals. Nevertheless, it is important to sketch at least a
brief outline of the typical movie studio procedures that generally
affect the content of an ordinary Soviet film.[1]

The procedure for soliciting synopses underwent a number of changes
during the period covered in this study (1917-1953), but in general the
first step was a meeting between a professional writer and some person
(studio official, film director, etc.) connected with the motion picture
industry. At this meeting, ideas were exchanged about the general subject matter of the proposed scenario and the development of the narrative
as well. During the first years of the Soviet regime, it was left to
the writers to select the political theme of the proposed film; some
writers were conscientious in their choice of the political theme, but
others considered it to be of secondary importance and merely injected
some political content into the story in a very arbitrary manner--just
to insure that the scenario would be politically acceptable.

Government officials in the Commissariat of Education soon began to
classify each film according to its political content, however, and developed a list of themes based on this classification. Thus, films were

---

[1]The following section is based mainly on Chapter II, "The Soviet
Studio," from the Soviet Film Industry, by Babitsky. This chapter draws
on his personal experience as a scenario-writer in Soviet film studios
from the mid-twenties until World War II. In addition, information about
the inner details of film studio operations was obtained from several
other sources, including an essay—in Russian—by Martin Lutich (another
former scenario-writer) published in New York by the Research Program on
the U.S.S.R. during 1953 as No. 31 in their Mimeographed Series. See
also Personal Interview No. 1313 of the Harvard University Refugee Interview Project; this interviewee was a Planning Economist and Bookkeeper
in a Soviet film studio from 1932 to 1942 and was interviewed in New York
City during 1950.

classified as Civil War pictures, anti-religious pictures, "history of the Revolutionary Movement" pictures and so on. Although these themes were developed at first merely to classify completed productions, it soon became the practice to publish a list of themes annually as a guide to future production. Thus, a scenario writer had to choose his theme from the list published each year. The list was revised annually to match the latest concerns of the political leadership and to commemorate significant anniversaries. In 1925, for example, it was decided to recommend the production of films about the Russian Revolution of 1905 in commemoration of the twentieth anniversary of this event; in 1927 the 1917 Revolution was to be featured in commemoration of its tenth anniversary; in 1929 themes of collectivization of agriculture and industrialization were stressed in conjunction with the new developments in those areas. Within these broad limits, however, the proposed writer still had considerable latitude in the choice of plot and treatment.

Having completed a synopsis, the writer submitted it for comment. During the 1920's, it was common to show the synopsis first to the scenario department of a film studio, where an editorial board reviewed it. During the 1940's many synopses were sent to a newly established Scenario Studio which specialized in the production of scenarios. (In addition, of course, the writer occasionally discussed his synopsis first with his personal acquaintances in the film industry, exercising some caution to protect his idea from plagiarism.) If and when the synopsis received approval, the author was commissioned to write a complete scenario. A contract was signed and the writer received an advance payment.

As soon as the first draft of a scenario had been completed by the writer, it was sent to the person who had commissioned it. Once more a discussion took place--with the result that a second draft was prepared to assimilate the suggestions made at this conference. Generally a number of persons took part in this and subsequent discussions of the script. These informal discussions provided ample opportunity for the exchange of ideas on specific points in the scenario, and a compromise had to be reached on all issues before the scenario received unqualified approval. After 1938 it became mandatory to submit all scenarios for approval to the centralized Scenario Department in the Main Administration for Art Films of the U.S.S.R. Committee on Film Affairs, in Moscow; the members of this Committee generally reviewed every scenario.

Once a scenario was approved, work began on a "shooting script" to be used by the film director. At this stage (which was called the "preparatory period") the writer submitted his work to the appropriate film director, who converted the scenario to suit his needs. Sometimes the film director worked alone; at other times he called on the author of the scenario for discussion. Again compromises were made and at this stage it was generally the writer who had to give ground. The well known and successful Soviet scenario writer, Evgeni Gabrilovich, once commented that "the complex relations between the writer and film director reflect a conflict of artistic tastes in which the writer is always the loser."[2] The film director, in turn, was forced to compromise by the members of

---

[2]Gabrilovich, E., "Pisatel' na fabrike" (The Writer in the Studio), Iskusstvo kino, 1936, Number 4, p. 44.

the editorial board of the studio's scenario department, which also reviewed the shooting script.

After much discussion, and considerable compromise, the studio was at last ready to begin filming. At this point, however, it was necessary to submit the compromise version of the shooting script to the Committee for Control of Repertory, a branch of the People's Commissariat of Education. (This review body had a number of predecessors with different names, such as the Film Art Council of the Political Education Section in the Commissariat of Education.) Despite all preceding revisions, many scenarios were disapproved at this stage; in 1925, for example, about 50 percent of scripts submitted for approval had to be revised further, and many of these were ultimately rejected.[3]

The ultimate result of the process of continual compromise was official approval of the shooting script. Now the work of filming could begin, but as soon as a few scenes had been filmed, they were exhibited to studio officials for discussion. Sometimes these preliminary shots were also exhibited to representatives of the professional association of film industry employees for criticism.[4] This procedure was repeated for longer sections of the motion picture. Finally, the completed film was reviewed and discussed by studio executives. During all these reviews, the director had to compromise. Next an informal discussion took place in the studio in the presence of the scenario writer, the film director, all the members of the studio's Art Council (which included other directors,

---

[3]Harper, S., Civic Training in Soviet Russia, Chicago, University of Chicago Press, 1929, p. 328.

[4]Eisenstein, "Foreword," Soviet Films 1938-9, Moscow, 1939, p. 2.

scenario writers, actors, cameramen, and technicians), as well as all Communist Party members employed in the studio, and some representatives of the local office of the governmental Motion Picture Administration.

This discussion of the completed film was generally "unofficial," despite the presence of so many persons, and was in sharp contrast to the "official" reviews which were to follow. At this stage the conversations were quite lively but friendly, because everyone knew everyone else well and also because all those participating in the discussion were equally responsible for the content of the film. The studio chief, who was always a member of the Communist Party but seldom an expert on motion picture production, bore general responsibility for all the films released by his studio. His deputy (generally someone with considerable experience in the motion picture industry) was considered to be equally responsible for the success of any picture. The Art Council, headed by the studio's Artistic Director (a party member) was particularly concerned with film content, as all its members were "creative" rather than "technical" employees. (The Art Council at the Leningrad Sovkino Studio, for example, consisted of two actors, one set designer, three directors, two cameramen and several scenario writers.[5]) The Communist Party members of the studio were considered to be responsible for the success of each film because of their political education and their knowledge of motion picture production. This was particularly true of the full-time Secretary of the studio's party organization, who always attended these discussions. The local office of the governmental Motion Picture Administration was

[5] Close Up, May, 1929, p. 96.

responsible for all film production, distribution, and exhibition in the area; of these activities, production was the most "politically sensitive" and representatives of this local office were invariably present at any review of a completed film before the picture was forwarded to headquarters for the official review.

The last opportunity for compromise and revision of the completed film was yet to come. Before the studio sent the film for official review, it was customary to invite an important Communist Party official to see the picture. This "guest" was usually an important political figure who could be relied on to reflect the current views of the Party leadership. In addition, this man was chosen because he would be frank and direct—but not "official" on this occasion. Therefore, additional changes could be made without arousing notice. If any doubts remained, the film officials would invite a second "guest"—a person connected with the top administrative body of the motion picture industry in Moscow—for additional discussion. Conversations with this person, too, were "unofficial" and quite frank.

All subsequent previews of the completed film were extremely formal. At the final review in the offices of the Committee for Control of Repertory—and the preview at the Film Club in Moscow—there was no opportunity for compromise; the scenario writer, director, and all others connected with the production had to accept "official" comments without question. If criticism was severe, "confessions" were expected—but most films passed the final hurdles successfully because of the many opportunities for compromise at earlier stages in the production process. The complex procedure for informal review usually accomplished its purpose: to assure the acceptance of a film by the political leadership.

The release of a film for distribution and exhibition usually attested to its acceptability to the Communist Party, but the film still had to prove itself with the Soviet audiences. The usual procedures for gauging public reaction were quite rudimentary. During the 1920's, some films were previewed for a group of industrial workers and comments were solicited.[6] Once in a while a film was also previewed in a rural area.[7] Neither of these "test" audiences could be relied on to reflect the preferences of the urban middle class (professional, semi-professional and white collar employees) who purchased a very substantial proportion of the movie tickets sold by commercial theaters.[8] Nevertheless, the opinions of these "working class" test audiences were "preferred" for political reasons, and some constructive ideas undoubtedly emerged from the discussions. During the 1920's, it was also fairly common to preview a new film for the members of an organization called "The Society of Friends of the Film." This organization had about 50,000 members, including "art lovers," persons connected with the film industry and ordinary workers.[9] Thus, changes were occasionally made in a film before its release to accommodate the views of a "test" audience.

---

[6]Bryher, W., Film Problems of Soviet Russia, 1929, p. 16.

[7]Eastman, F., "Motion Pictures in Russia," Christian Century, Volume 53, September 9, 1936, p. 1186.

[8]Estimates for the year 1940, obtained from 2,465 former Soviet citizens (who filled out questionnaires prepared by Harvard University's Refugee Interview Project) indicate that 45 percent of the semi-professional and white collar employees said they attended movies "frequently" (usually once a week), whereas only 33 percent of the skilled workers, 29 percent of the semi-skilled and 12 percent of the unskilled workers reported going "frequently" to the movies in the Soviet Union. See Chapter 7.

[9]"The Cinema Industry in the U.S.S.R.," Soviet Union Review, April 1929, p. 55; Freeman, J., An American Testament, 1936, pp. 585-88.

Scenarios and films scheduled for production were sometimes altered on the basis of the success or failure of films previously released. Studio administrators obtained box office statistics for the latest releases and, on the basis of these data, made changes in films still in production. Priorities were juggled in response to variations in popularity of the pictures released during the previous year. As Babitsky points out:

> When a filmed version of a fiction classic proved successful with Soviet audiences, administrators immediately ordered studios to accelerate production of pictures based on Russian classics. Soon afterwards, when a historical film found favor, the Moscow authorities, forgetting their recent directive, would insist on priorities for historical scenarios. Writers submitting a completed work of the type no longer in vogue encountered a chilly reception in the studios and were advised to switch immediately to historical themes. In the meantime administrators were preparing new directives, and the procedure would be repeated over and over again.[10]

It would be difficult to determine whether Babitsky exaggerates the sensitivity of studio executives, but there is no doubt that trends in audience preferences were closely watched and that they had a profound effect on the content of films in production.

Other Occasions for Compromise

In addition to the frequent meetings and discussions that occurred during the production of a particular film, there were other occasions when film industry administrators, artists and audiences exchanged opinions and attempted to compromise conflicting points of view. Many opinions and attitudes were gradually modified over a period of years as

---

[10]Babitsky, Soviet Film Industry, p. 101.

a result of this continuing interchange of ideas, and individuals who had been adamant in discussions of a particular film frequently softened their own prejudices and preferences between the time one film was released and work on the next picture began. Among the most important of these opportunities for compromise were the meetings and publications which concerned the motion picture industry. In this connection, trade unions and professional associations played an important role because they frequently sponsored meetings and concerned themselves with the development of an active trade press.

During the first decade of the Soviet regime, the practice of discussing motion pictures at meetings was not very common in the film studio, but such discussions took place nevertheless under the sponsorship of numerous organizations (such as the Association for the Revolutionary Film) to which many of the creative personnel belonged. These meetings, which were quite informal, provided a platform for the various "schools," and both foreign as well as domestic productions were examined from the standpoint of content, style, popular acceptance, and so on. A few Communist Party officials, such as the Commissar of Education, Lunacharski, participated in these discussions, but in general the viewpoint of the Party's top leaders did not receive authoritative expression because the "official line" had not yet sufficiently developed. Therefore, nearly everyone attempted to express a Communist viewpoint, but nobody spoke with finality. Although there was considerable controversy, all points of view were given consideration and the exchange of ideas was free and thorough. In the absence of a single, authoritative Communist "line," everyone felt free to draw his own conclusions and to develop his own views on style and film content.

Official statements about film content, from political leaders, remained quite general throughout the 1920's. Most Soviet productions were mildly criticized, but the majority of films eventually passed all censorship—and even the most severe official criticism seldom resulted in the banning of a completed motion picture. Nevertheless, the Party gave special support and encouragement to those directors and scenario writers who identified themselves most closely with the Communist Party. Two groups in particular—the Association for the Revolutionary Film, and the Society of Friends of the Soviet Film—were encouraged to organize film personnel and to assure the expression of a Communist point of view at all times. These organizations attempted to carry out their aims by means of meetings and publications for the film industry.

As early as 1924, the Association for the Revolutionary Film organized discussion groups in Moscow and Leningrad.[11] Membership in the Association for the Revolutionary Film was limited to persons actually engaged in motion picture work. To obtain the views of "outsiders," the Association helped to organize the Society of Friends of the Soviet Film. In a declaration signed by Kuleshov, Lebedev, Eisenstein, and others, published on February 26, 1924, the Association urged that a Society of Friends of the Soviet Film be organized to draw spectators into the discussion of films.[12] The Association and the Society held joint meetings to discuss film content.[13] By 1928, the Association had branches in

---

[11] Lebedev, N., Ocherk istorii kino SSSR (Outline of the History of the Movie in the USSR), Moscow, Goskinoizdat, Volume 1, 1947, p. 90.

[12] Ibid.

[13] Freeman, J., Voices of October, 1930, p. 261.

several other cities—wherever film production was taking place.[14]

In the year 1928, when the Communist Party undertook a "crash program" to collectivize farms and to build up heavy industry, more determined efforts were made to exercise ideological control in the arts. In
this connection, the first Communist Party Conference on Film Questions
was convened in March, 1928. Spokesmen for the Party reiterated the
statements that had been made at the Twelfth Party Congress (April 1923)
and the Thirteenth Party Congress (May, 1924): that Party control over
the film industry was inadequate, that film industry personnel should be
Party members, and that film content ought to be more thoroughly reviewed
by censorship officials.[15] The speakers at the First Party Conference
on Film Questions were not writers, or directors, or other "creative"
artists, but Party functionaries and Government officials; artists were
not asked to express their views—they were told what to think. The
speeches were more detailed than previous party statements on the subject
of film content, but they still abounded in generalities—"films must be
used for propaganda," "films must be made for industrial workers and
peasants," and so on.[16] Communist Party spokesmen refrained from dictating specific rules on the subject of film content and individual films
were not discussed in any detail.

From 1928 until 1932, the Association for the Revolutionary Film
undertood to speak for the Communist Party in all matters pertaining to
film content. The Association attempted to dictate to all film artists

[14]Harper, S., Civic Training in Soviet Russia, 1929, p. 336.

[15]Ibid., pp. 334-35.   [16]Ibid.

and to bring about a "proletarian" trend in film production. The Association organized frequent meetings and used them to criticize those artists who attempted to adhere to their individual views on film content. Dissenters were permitted to speak only if they were prepared to "confess" their errors. These meetings therefore were organized in advance and carefully controlled—in contrast to the informal discussions that had taken place before 1928.

In 1932 Communist Party leaders decided to abolish the dictatorship of the Association for the Revolutionary Film and to replace it with the Union of Film and Photography Workers. The new Union was not permitted to exercise much influence on the film industry and its personnel, but it did conduct occasional meetings to discuss film content. Many other such meetings took place, however, under the auspices of individual film studios, as the Communist Party decided to concentrate greater powers in the hands of film studio executives and officials of the nationwide Film Administration that operated the motion picture industry on behalf of the Soviet Government. From 1932 on, nearly all meetings were controlled by Communist Party officials who exercised this control on all occasions— meetings of studio personnel, meetings of the Union of Film and Photography Workers, and so on. Each meeting that was concerned with film content enabled those in attendance to hear the "party line" in great detail. Specific films were discussed and analyzed. Pictures that were especially liked by high Communist leaders—such as "Counter-plan" (1932) and "Chapayev" (1934)—were held up as models, while numerous other films were severely criticized in every detail. Artists were required to speak about their films for the benefit of other artists, as well as for their own benefit, with the aim of improving the quality of film content in accordance with Communist Party requirements. Thus, film artists participated in the evaluation of films not only during the production process but also at all other times. Meetings therefore served the purpose of confronting the film artist with political demands pertaining to his work.

Because artists were required to participate at all meetings, however, they continued to make their views known to other artists and Party officials. In this way administrators and officials learned more about art. Some writers and film directors dared to speak with great conviction about their work, and even to criticize government and Party officials, usually in a veiled manner. While criticism of the highest Communist leaders was not permitted, "constructive criticism" of lesser politicians and officials was sometimes tolerated. Some artists complained about bureaucratic mismanagement in the studios, in the film industry's training schools, and in the government's Film Administration. Artists chose their words carefully, of course, but it was usually evident that they were dissatisfied with film industry officials from time to time, and these dissatisfactions were voiced at numerous meetings. Thus, for example, Eisenstein spoke in great detail about his views on film art at the January 1935 Conference in Moscow. He complained that the publishers of the government newspaper Izvestiya had distorted his views by editing an article written by Eisenstein for publication in that paper.[17] He also criticized the film "Counter-plan," which had been held up as a

---

[17]Seton, M., Eisenstein, New York, A. A. Wyn, 1952, p. 332.

model by Communist leaders. Finally Eisenstein charged that the only
result of the "suppression of one creative individual by another" would
be the destruction of talent, and for this statement he was applauded by
the audience.[18]

Some of the most severe criticism of film industry administrators
came from professional writers. Unlike the cameramen and film directors
who were employed full-time in the film industry, writers often were
more independent because some of their income came from other sources:
books, magazines, the theater, radio and television. Consequently, meetings of the Union of Soviet Writers often provided a platform for writers
to voice their dissatisfaction with conditions in the motion picture industry. At a meeting of the Union of Soviet Writers on August 29, 1951,
for example, the chief administrative official of the film industry,
the Minister Ivan Bolshakov, was sharply criticized. He was accused of
submitting plans which disregarded the interests of writers.[19] This
criticism was expressed at a meeting, but was subsequently published, too,
to gain a wider audience.

Like meetings, publications played an important role in the communication of points of view and the interchange of ideas. Many articles on
the subject of film content appeared frequently in the major Soviet newspapers and magazines, and specialized trade journals also were published
with great regularity. While some space was devoted to technical subjects and statistics, most of the published material concerned film content. Articles were contributed not only by professional writers, but

[18]Ibid., p. 349.

[19]Literaturnaya gazeta, September 1, 1951, p. 3.

also by film directors, actors, cameramen, and film industry executives. Within the industry, these publications had a wide audience--and some "outsiders" read them as well.

As early as 1924, at least five different newspapers and magazines were devoted exclusively to films. The Association for the Revolutionary Film published a magazine. The Society of the Friends of the Soviet Film published a newspaper. The "Proletkult," a group devoted to the spread of "proletarian culture," published a film magazine. Two film studios jointly issued a weekly magazine devoted to films. The People's Commissariat of Education published a periodical on the subject of films for children. Most of these magazines and newspapers were issued through a publishing house in Moscow which specialized in film and theater literature. While the names of these publications changed from time to time, they continued to appear until the early 1930's. As the film industry became more centralized, the number of periodicals declined, but the subject of film content continued to predominate on the pages of these publications. In addition, entire books on the subject of Soviet films began to appear and collections of selected magazine and newspaper articles were also published in book form. The accumulation of printed materials led to the establishment of several specialized libraries on the film industry and stimulated scholarly research on the history and evolution of motion pictures.

Although the majority of articles and books echoed the current "party line," there was still room for original thought (carefully phrased) in most of the publications that dealt with the film. Artists as well as administrators wrote much of the material pertaining to film content in

the trade publications, although professional film critics predominated
in other newspapers and magazines. Virtually all published material
about films was carefully read by film industry personnel. Published
articles stimulated many private discussions and even rejoinders that
also found their way into pages of the trade publications. Thus, differences of opinion between two or more persons were sometimes aired before the eyes of thousands of readers concerned with the subject of the
controversy. These written debates occurred not only between artists
but also between artists and administrative officials. In 1948, for
example, the noted film director Pudovkin penned these thoughts on the
relation of planning to creativity:

> In a field such as Art, where opportunity for unhampered expres-
> sion of creative individuality is indispensable to the artist,
> a plan cannot be a mere enumeration of orders placed by one or
> several organizations, nor can it be drawn up by some superior
> authority in charge of art affairs, and then turned over to
> producers and directors for exact and unquestioning fulfillment.
> . . . This would be a bureaucratic system, undesirable and im-
> possible in Art."[20]

As previously indicated, writers were often the most severe critics
of the motion picture administration. This criticism often appeared on
the pages of the newspaper published by the Union of Soviet Writers,
called Literaturnaya gazeta. The motion picture industry's own publications also had professional writers on their editorial boards, however,
and these artists—together with film directors, cameramen, actors, and
so on—saw to it that different points of view were expressed on the
pages of these publications. Sometimes they went too far and were

---

[20]Pudovkin, V., Soviet Historical Films, Moscow, All-Union Society
for Cultural Relations with Foreign Countries, 1948, p. 10.

deposed. In 1946 for instance, the editor-in-chief of the publication
Iskusstvo kino (Art of the Film) was dismissed on orders from the Film
Ministry because the magazine had published an article by Eisenstein
that allegedly advocated "art for art's sake."[21] Even after this episode, some artists continued to contribute to the pages of this and
other publications and found a wide audience for their views in the
motion picture industry. As a result, newspapers and magazines continued
to play an important role in the exchange and modification of ideas pertaining to film content.

---

[21]New York Times, September 23, 1946.

CHAPTER IX

FILM PRODUCTION AND CONTENT

"The Soviet film industry could produce 500-600 pictures a year if low-quality films were wanted."
                    --USSR Film Minister Bol'shakov, in Pravda, June 28, 1949

More than 20 films were produced in Russia in the year of 1918. Although the Communists had carried out their seizure of power the previous year, several years of civil war took place before Lenin's regime was able to control the remnants of the former Russian empire. The weakness of the Soviet regime during 1918 was reflected in the virtual absence of propaganda in films produced that year. As the Civil War continued, production of feature films practically stopped. The supplies of raw film stock required for motion picture production disappeared, as there were no raw film factories in Russia at all, and imports from Western Europe had stopped. After the Civil War, when Lenin proclaimed a "new economic policy" to encourage the resumption of private enterprise and commerce, raw film stock was again imported and the production of Soviet feature films under Communist auspices began to take place in Moscow, Leningrad and several other film producing centers.

The first Soviet feature productions reflected the disrupted state of the motion picture industry in Soviet Russia. Several years were required to re-establish the routines of film production, from the development of a scenario to the final review of a completed film. Nevertheless, film makers worked in an optimistic frame of mind because movie theaters throughout Soviet Russia revived quickly from the chaos of the Civil War period (as soon as the import of foreign feature films resumed) and also because Lenin had declared in 1921 that "for us, the film is the most important of all arts."

1923-1928

Twelve full-length feature films were produced during the fiscal year 1922-23, more than three times that number were released by Soviet studios during the following year, and production rose each year during "NEP"—the period of the New Economic Policy.[1] These early Soviet pictures clearly reflected all three of the viewpoints which had a profound influence on the content of Soviet films: the political demand for propaganda, the artistic demand for creativity, and the spectators' demand for entertainment. Each film was a "mix" of these three elements. In some pictures, the political element stood out; in other pictures artistic experimentation dominated, and in others the entertainment aspect was paramount—but every picture reflected all three viewpoints. Each film was a compromise between the three definitions of the purpose of a motion picture. Some typical films will be described to illustrate the three elements of film content, and to demonstrate that these elements were present at all times, even though the volume of Soviet film production fluctuated in various time-periods between 1918 and 1952.

---

[1]Lebedev, N., Ocherk istorii kino SSSR (Outline of the History of the Movie in the U.S.S.R.), Moscow, Goskinoizdat, Vol. 1, 1947, p. 87.

The films described in this chapter are "typical" because they are quite similar to hundreds of other Soviet motion-pictures in most respects. The 26 films which are described here were selected for description because they are just a little more political (or artistic, or entertaining) than the "average" Soviet film. Thus, they illustrate more clearly the nature of political (or artistic, or entertaining) content to be found in Soviet motion-pictures. To the extent that the "mix" of politics, art and entertainment in particular films is not wholly in balance, the task of illustrating these elements of the "mix" is simplified. Therefore, these 26 films are not altogether typical, because the mix of three basic ingredients is slightly out of balance in each film; but they readily illustrate the political, artistic and entertaining elements of all Soviet film content.

Political Content

Typical of the early films with considerable political content was the picture "Little Red Devils" (1923). This picture was based on a script by a Communist Party member who later became the head of the Chief Repertory Committee (that is, the government committee charged with the responsibility of reviewing all completed films prior to their release for public exhibition). Thus, the scenario-writer clearly understood the "Party line" better than most other artists, and his loyalty to the Party was evident. The film director, on the other hand, was not a Party member—but a man with some experience in motion picture production before the Revolution. Their joint effort was a film which not only met political and artistic standards, but also pleased motion picture audiences. The former Soviet scenario-writer Babitsky described "Little

Red Devils" as "the first popular Soviet film" and noted that it "satisfied the spectators and received lavish praise from Party reviewers."[2]
The American political scientist Samuel Harper, traveling in the Soviet
Union during the summer of 1926, observed that "Little Red Devils" was
"one of the most popular films."[3] The film derived much of its popular
appeal from its youthful cast, particularly a six-year-old boy who was
described by one foreign correspondent as "a natural comic."[4]

The subject matter of the film was the military campaign of a Red
Army unit against a counter-revolutionary force (headed by a military
commander named Makhno) during the Civil War. The Red Army unit happened to be a cavalry group commanded by the dashing Communist Commander
Budenni, and much of the drama stemmed from the cavalry battle scenes—
but the feature attraction was the little group of scouts that assisted
the Red Army unit. The scouts consisted of a young Russian boy and his
sister, later joined by a Negro youth. (The Negro was supposed to sym-
bolize the alliance between the Russian proletariat and the colored
colonial people of Africa and Asia.) The film thus combined propaganda,
art, and entertainment in skillful fashion.

Artistic Content

Although a number of film makers experimented with film content and
technique, many of the artists who had worked in the pre-revolutionary
Russian movie industry chose to imitate the style of the pre-Communist

_____

[2]Babitsky, P., Soviet Film Industry, 1955, p. 117.

[3]Harper, S., Civic Training in Soviet Russia, 1929, p. 43.

[4]Evans, E., "The Soviet Idea in the 'Kino,'" Asia, August 1926,
p. 733.

film. Those film makers who deviated from the pre-revolutionary style, however, frequently exceeded even the most radical experimenters in Germany, France, Italy, and the United States in their search for new and original forms of artistic expression. The most dramatic experiments occurred in the period 1926-1928, but some of the films produced before 1926 revealed the tremendous interest (among artists) in new forms of artistic expression on the screen. At first, some Russian film artists looked to the West for inspiration and for specific examples of new styles. The American cowboy film, for example, was welcomed both by Soviet audiences and film artists as a refreshingly different type of motion picture.

The Soviet film called "The Extraordinary Adventures of Mr. West in the Land of the Bolsheviks" (1924) was a skillful combination of satire and the cowboy drama. Unlike the typical American cowboy film, which based its appeal on serious dramatic episodes, this Soviet picture was essentially a comedy. The humor resulted from the confusion in the mind of Senator West, the central character who misunderstood the facts of Soviet life. The comedy of errors served political ends because it illustrated the anti-Communist hostility of the foreign press, and the naivete of "capitalist" politicians. Senator West was a fool who believed that the Soviet population was "uncivilized" as the American Indian. Therefore, Senator West hired a cowboy to be his bodyguard when he went to Russia. On his arrival "in the land of the Bolsheviks" he fell victim to the cynical and sinister tricks of a gang of "counter-revolutionaries" who exploited his misconceptions (about Russia) to their advantage in a series of episodes that ridiculed Mr. West while amusing the Soviet film audience. At the end of the picture, Mr. West was rescued from his captors and learned to appreciate the bolshevik way of life. Thus, this picture combined a political attack on capitalists with artistic innovations (the synthesis of satire with the American cowboy style), while providing entertainment to Soviet audiences who enjoyed watching both the fool and the cowboy.

A more extreme experiment in film art was the picture "Strike" (1925). The director, Eisenstein, had previously conducted radical experiments in the Soviet theater, but this motion picture about a factory workers' strike was his first attempt to introduce innovations in the film medium. The scenario for this picture deliberately minimized a conventional plot, substituting "images of collective action."[5] The characters remained namelss; there was merely "a union organizer," "a worker," "a company spy," and "a foreman." These characters were depicted as "types" rather than individuals, and the most important role was assigned to the mass of working men. The workers constituted the main focus of the film; their attempts to organize themselves, their decision to strike, and their suffering at the hands of the police overshadowed the role of any single individual. Towards the end of the film, Eisenstein experimented for the first time with violent "montage" in an attempt to intensify the impact of the final scene in which soldiers shoot down the striking workers. The slaughter of the workers was compared to a bull being butchered, as follows:

> The butcher moves past the camera (panning) swinging his bloody rope.
> A crowd runs to a fence, breaks through it, and hides behind it (in two or three shots).

---

[5]Seton, M., Eisenstein, 1952, p. 68.

Arms fall into the frame (film-frame).
The head of the bull is severed from the trunk.
A Volley (of bullets).
Soldiers' feet walk away from the camera.
Blood floats on the water, discoloring it.
(Close-up) Blood gushes from the slit throat of the bull.
Blood is pouring from a basin (held by hands) into a pail.
Dissolve from a truck loaded with pails of blood to a passing
truck loaded with scrap-iron.
The bull's tongue is pulled through the slit throat (to prevent
the convulsions from damaging the tongue).
The soldiers' feet walk away from the camera (seen at a further
distance than previously).
The bull's skin is stripped off.
1,500 bodies (lie) at the foot of the cliff.
Two skinned bulls' heads.
A hand lying in a pool of blood.
(Close-up) Filling the entire screen: the eye of a dead bull.
(Title) THE END.[6]

Entertainment Content

A number of motion pictures produced during the period 1921-1924
were made primarily for entertainment. This type of film was frequently
based on a pre-revolutionary novel, play or folk-tale. Although political
considerations influenced the choice of topic, there was seldom any attempt
to re-write the story or to tamper with the plot for political reasons.
The artistry of these motion pictures was of a high quality—particularly
because talented actors were usually borrowed from the stage—but very
little effort was made to translate the novel or play into a work of film
art; rather the end product was lacking in experimentation because the
artists chose to imitate the conventions of the stage and the producers
were satisfied to recreate rather than to create a work of art. Therefore, the outstanding feature of these films was their popular appeal:
the subject matter was invariably popular, the cast was popular and the

[6]Ibid., p. 69.

treatment was merely a repeat performance (this time, on film) of works of art which had demonstrated their popularity years ago.

A good example of this type of entertainment film was the picture "Collegiate Registrar" (1925), based on Pushkin's story The Station-master. The film, which hewed to the line of Pushkins's tale, depicted a poor widower who is deserted by his only child. At the beginning of the story, the manager of a station along the highway ekes out a miserable living by providing fresh horses to travelers. His only joy in life is his lovely daughter. The stationmaster finds himself completely alone when his daughter elopes to the capital city of St. Petersburg; while she is enjoying life in the capital her father dies of grief. Later the daughter stops by to see his grave, but immediately returns to her pleasant life in St. Petersburg.

Another film with audience appeal was based on the play "Aelita" by Count Alexei N. Tolstoi. The film, released in 1924, combined scenes of contemporary Soviet life with a fantastic space trip to the planet Mars. At the beginning of the film the engineer Los is hard at work. Next he is seen in a rocket ship accompanied by a Red Army soldier and a detective. Landing on Mars, they find themselves in the midst of a political revolution. The engineer Los also manages to have a love affair with the queen of Mars, named Aelita. At the end of the film, Los "comes back to earth" to discover that it was all just a dream.[7]

Films of this type were extremely popular in the Soviet Union.[8] In

[7]Babitsky, P., Soviet Film Industry, 1955, pp. 119-20.

[8]Macdonald, D., "Soviet Society and its Cinema," Partisan Review, Winter, 1939, p. 91.

addition, they were the first films to be exported abroad. The lack of propaganda, the artistry of the production, and the drama of the story had great appeal in the West.[9] In this way, the Soviet government obtained precious foreign currency and depicted the Soviet Union as a land of culture. Therefore, the Soviet government encouraged the production of this type of film.

1929-1933

Following Lenin's death, a struggle for power developed within the Communist Party. Only after Stalin had defeated his rival Trotsky did the new Communist chieftain undertake an economic program involving major reforms in agriculture and industry. Thus the year 1929 witnessed the tremendous effort to "collectivize" the farmers on the basis of the kolkhoz (collective farm) system. Immediately after this agricultural reform had been introduced, Stalin also reorganized Soviet industry and laid down the first Five-Year-Plan, intending to accelerate the production of tools and the erection of factories. To facilitate these enormous undertakings, virtually every aspect of Soviet life underwent changes. The film industry was no exception. The administrative organization charged with the control of film production, distribution, and exhibition was reorganized in 1930, with a new administrative head, Shumyatski.

As a consequence of reorganization, personnel changes, economic upheaval and the introduction of sound into film-making, the production of Soviet films "turned the corner" between 1929 and 1930 and fell off sharply during 1931-1933. The dramatic decline in output was due, in part, to a demand for increased political propaganda about the kolkhoz

[9]Carter, H., The New Spirit in the Russian Theatre, 1929, p. 289.

and the Five-Year-Plan. To some extent, film artists resisted the
effort to dictate themes and content. At the same time, film audiences
began to grow tired of the huge dose of propaganda (in literature and
on the radio as well as in the film and theater) about the reforms in
agriculture and industry; the decision to halt imports of foreign entertainment films at this time also made Soviet audiences restive and created a greater demand for entertainment films produced in Soviet studios.
Consequently Soviet films continued to be artistic and entertaining,
despite some increase in propaganda content and a decided fall in the
volume of production.

Political Content

A number of films produced between 1929 and 1933 were concerned
chiefly with the reforms in agriculture and industry, but other political
themes also flourished. The film "Judas" (1930) had an anti-religious
theme. Judas is a holy man preaching "non-resistance" to the peasants
during the Civil War. The holy man convinces some pro-Communist peasants
to lay down their arms, which results in their slaughter by anti-Communist
forces. Although Judas later admits his guilt, the head of the monastery
continues to support the anti-Communist soldiers to the very end.[10]

Another political theme sponsored by the Communist party concerned
the evils of racial prejudice--particularly in the United States. Several
films in this vein were produced during the period 1929-33; the tenor of
these films is well illustrated by "Black and White," a film never

---

[10]New York Times, February 16, 1930, Section III, p. 8. See also
Close Up, October 1929, p. 316 and November 1930, pp. 329-32.

completed because the election of Roosevelt in 1932 promised diplomatic recognition of the Soviet Union by the United States and the anti-American overtones resulted in a ban on this picture at the last moment. Nevertheless this film is fairly typical, and detailed descriptions of the scenario were made public by American Negroes who had been invited to Russia to act in the film.

Langston Hughes was one of the Americans who went to Russia to produce "Black and White" in 1932. He described the proposed scenario as follows: A union organizer attempts to enroll Negroes in the steel workers' union. He is opposed by poor whites, the factory managers, and "absentee Yankee capitalists." A race riot starts in Birmingham, Alabama, and the "rich Negroes who own radio stations" broadcast a plea for help to the North—but the Northern "liberals" will do nothing. The plea for aid is also heard by union members in the North, however, who promptly go to Alabama in buses "to save their Negro brothers."[11]

Artistic Content

The film directors, cameramen, actors, and other artists continued to strive for original works of art despite the frequent criticism of "formalistic experiments" during the years 1929-1933. The creativity of the Soviet artists would not be denied. Thus, in the film "Alone" (1931) the producers brilliantly created emotional moods by means of photographic techniques. The story concerns a city girl who is assigned to a remote Siberian village as a school teacher, where she finds herself alone among

---

[11]Hughes, L., <u>I Wonder as I Wander</u>, 1956, pp. 78-80.

the shepherds who are strangers to her. When she overcomes her fears
and lends moral support to the poor shepherds in a controversy with the
rich ones, she is kidnapped and abandoned in the snow to die—but saved
at last in a dramatic airplane rescue. During the entire picture, black,
white and shades of gray were used effectively to set the mood: white
(dishes, clothing, buildings and linens) suggest optimism and happiness,
while dark images and sombre black objects were emphasized in certain
scenes to convey feelings of anxiety and sadness.[12]

Another work of art was the film "Earth" (1930), a picture that pre-
tended to depict the introduction of the kolkhoz system but actually
glorified the "old ways" of peasant life—particularly the labor of the
Ukrainian farmer and the fertility of his land. Although the collective
farm obtains a tractor, it is seen arriving for the first time in the
midst of a bountiful harvest produced entirely without the help of machinery. By means of his great creative artistry, the film director
Dovzhenko expressed a moving lament for the old way of life as it faded
away before the reforms of Stalin.[13]

Entertainment Content

The popular demand for entertainment, which refused to be denied by
the curtailment of film imports from the West, expressed itself clearly
at the box office and resulted in the production of a number of entertaining Soviet films during the years 1929-1933. Three short stories by
Anton Chekhov were combined in the film "Ranks and People" (1929) because

[12]New York Times, September 13, 1931, Section IX, p. 5.

[13]Babitsky, P., Soviet Film Industry, pp. 147-48.

of their common thread: each depicted the influence of rank and social
status on man's perception of reality. In the story called <u>Chameleon</u>,
two policemen find a vicious dog and decide to shoot it on the spot
until someone suggests that the dog belongs to a high-ranking army
officer. A long discussion follows, characterized by changes of opinion
which fluctuate faster than a chameleon can change colors. In <u>The Anna
Cross</u>, Chekhov tells about a low-ranking civil servant who marries a
beautiful, but poor, orphan girl; her beauty attracts the attention of
several high-ranking officials, who reward the husband with a promotion
and a medal while enjoying the favors of his flirtatious wife. The
third story, <u>Death of a Civil Servant</u>, tells about another poor man who
is so flustered by a trivial accident involving an important official
that he literally apologizes himself to death.

Another entertaining film was the picture "Road to Life" (1931)
which was so charming and sentimental that it enjoyed great success not
only in the Soviet Union but also in the United States. Like some European films produced after the second World War, it concerns a group of
homeless boys, recently orphaned, who are re-educated at a Home for
Boys under the guidance of a youth leader. The boy Mustafa, a real tough
kid, is rounded up with his gang after they kill a woman in a brawl; the
police ask him: "What do you want most?" The little boy replies: "Candy,
vodka, and a girl!" The gang is tempted with cigarettes to enter the
Boys' Town but the thief "Bet Your Life" tries to win them back to their
criminal ways and eventually murders Mustafa. His death convinces the
rest of the gang to repent and to make themselves into good Soviet citizens.[14]

----

[14]Rotha, P., <u>The Film Till Now</u>, 1949, p. 564.

1934-1940

Following the very demanding tempo of collectivization of agriculture and the first Five-Year-Plan, it became apparent that the tempo could not be maintained indefinitely. Nevertheless a second Five-Year-Plan was launched and then a third one—but the tempo declined (at least temporarily) as Stalin announced that "life will be more pleasant." The note of optimism was soon drowned out, however, by the intensive purges of "enemies of the people" in industry, the army, the police, the government administration and the Communist Party. Then, in 1939, a major war began in Europe, and the fiasco in Finland underscored the need for strengthening the military position of the Soviet Union.

In the Soviet film industry, production of feature films again "turned the corner" in 1934 and increased briefly—then rose and fell from year to year in an erratic fashion—never approaching the volume achieved during the 1920's. The film industry administration was purged in 1937. After Shumyatski was executed as "an enemy of the people," a police official named Semeon Dukel'ski was appointed chief administrator of the motion picture industry, but he was soon replaced by an administrator named Bolshakov. Simultaneously the entire administrative apparatus of the Soviet motion picture industry underwent several organizational changes: the structure devised in 1930 and revised in 1933 was changed again in 1936 and again in 1938. Despite these changes, however, the motion picture industry as a whole continued to grow in productive capacity and exhibition facilities. The number of industry employees increased and the size of the audience grew. Both the artists and the audiences continued to demand recognition of their interests. Therefore, Soviet films continued to feature art and entertainment as well as political propaganda.

Political Content

In addition to the standard political themes typical of Soviet films, the pictures produced between 1934 and 1940 contained some new propaganda elements. Outstanding among these was the glorification of leaders of the Communist Party in the Soviet Union. The film "Lenin in 1918" (1939) depicted both Lenin and Stalin, although many of those who had been prominent among the party leadership in 1918 were absent from the film--just as they were now absent from the political scene. The film tells of "a conspiracy to assassinate Lenin"; many of Stalin's political rivals, including Trotsky, Bukharin, Zinovyev, Kamenev and others were implicated in the plot. Stalin was depicted as being far away from Moscow at the time of the assassination attempt, but on hand to greet Lenin after his recovery. Thus entire films were devoted to pseudo-historical chronicles of the activities of Communist Party leaders. In addition to Lenin, films were devoted to Kirov (the late party leader in Leningrad) and Sverdlov, among others. All these films combined selected historical facts with fictitious episodes, and real persons with fictitious characters.

Artistic Content

During the period 1934-40, works of film art continued to appear as in previous periods. Some derived their inspiration from literary classics; others were entirely original creations in the film medium. Although some creative efforts were ultimately banned, the administrators of the motion picture industry were not hostile to art as such. The film "Childhood of Maksim Gorki" (1938) is an example of skillful use of the film medium to translate Gorki's autobiography into visual terms. The film combines excellent acting, careful direction, and masterful photography to re-create the childhood environment of the famous Russian writer. All of Gorki's skill in depicting characters and situations is faithfully reflected in the film.

The picture called "Alexander Nevski" (1938), by Eisenstein, his first completed work since his return from the West in the early 1930's, revealed frequent glimpses of his creativity. Supplemented by an original musical score composed by Sergei Prokofyev, Eisenstein's work again demonstrates his mastery of crowds and his great sense of drama. The episode of "The Battle on the Ice" is particularly impressive. At the same time, the film clearly shows that Eisenstein was forced to compromise with the political authorities, particularly in the way he had to glorify the role of Alexander Nevski. A compromise with audience preferences is also apparent, especially in the touches of humor (missing from his earlier films) and the deliberate pace of the action (which is in sharp contrast to the erratic and shock-producing tempo of his earlier films such as "The Battleship Potyomkin" and "October"). Despite the more conventional treatment of subject matter, however, the film is still a work of art.

Entertainment Content

The period 1934-1940 saw the release of several films about romance, music and sports, despite the atmosphere of purges and war preparations. The film "Volga--Volga" (1938), named after a popular song first introduced in this picture, tells the story of a simple girl whose talents

as a composer of songs almost goes unrecognized. She has to overcome
bureaucratic opposition to win the chance to enter her composition in a
music contest, but her efforts are crowned with success and her gifts
are recognized. After hearing her popular tune (and the artistic creations of other amateurs as well) the little bureaucrat sheepishly
admits that "we have so much talent!" The picture is a convenient
vehicle for light music, dancing and some slapstick comedy, and manages
to avoid anything very serious. The director of this film distinguished
himself in a number of such productions during the period 1934-40, but
he was by no means the only one who contributed such entertaining films
to the Soviet screen at that time. Thus, film audiences could reason-
ably expect to be diverted and entertained by the film-makers who never
lost sight of the box office.

1941-1945

Hitler's decision to invade the Soviet Union in June of 1941 was
predicated on the assumption that German troops would reach Moscow before
the end of the year, and the Germans made every effort to achieve this
aim. Although the Germans failed to reach their goal, their forces advanced very rapidly through the western territory of the Soviet Union,
causing chaos in the Soviet war economy and armed forces. The Soviet
Government was able to evacuate men, supplies and equipment to the East,
however, as part of the strategy which assumed that Hitler could be
stopped eventually just as Napoleon had been stopped. The decision to
move the Soviet centers of power eastward required that priority be given
to the most essential men, supplies, and equipment. One of the industries

that was relocated was the motion picture industry. The studios at Kiev,
Leningrad, Moscow, and Odessa were shifted eastward during 1941, and film
production continued throughout the war.

Concerning film content, the Party line shifted dramatically from
the "capitalism vs. communism" theme to the "Germany vs. Russia" theme.
This shift did not come about merely because Stalin's brand of communism
lacked supporters among the Soviet population, but also because a strict
interpretation of class consciousness and class warfare would have in-
hibited a determined resistance to the German invasion, insofar as the
average Soviet citizen was confronted by the average German fighting man
rather than the "evil German capitalists" or Hitler personally. To defeat the "little men" who were overrunning the Soviet Union, it was
absolutely necessary to stress the fact that they were Germans, because
they were obviously not wealthy capitalists—merely "victims" of the
capitalistic system. Since the sentiment of pity might weaken the war
effort of the Soviet people, the revised Communist Party line demanded
hatred of the enemy. To propagate this sentiment of hatred for Germans,
a massive propaganda campaign was deemed absolutely necessary by the
Communist Party and the film industry administration was adamant in demanding that hatred for the enemy should be cultivated; nevertheless, the
content of films produced during the war period clearly indicates that
some other themes were still tolerated. The popular demand for entertainment did not disappear, although it diminished somewhat because of
the serious business of war; the Soviet government found it convenient
to appease the popular hunger for entertainment by importing musical
comedies and other gay, diverting films from Hollywood. Therefore the

Soviet studios could concentrate primarily on the production of serious films, while Hollywood filled much of the demand for amusement.

As for the artists' perpetual desire for self-expression and creative effort, these were still tolerated to a degree because the artist was indispensable. Nevertheless even the artist found himself overwhelmed by the horrors of war and therefore diminished the expressive ego needs somewhat, in favor of the need to survive. Especially at the beginning of the war, when victory was in doubt, films were produced in great haste, with little attention to detail. Subtlety virtually disappeared, replaced by inartistic crudities——a "black and white" expression of the issues and the personalities. Art returned, however, as soon as there was a basis for it. By the end of the war, when victory was near, the artist again returned to his favorite role and a number of striking films resulted.

Thus, in wartime, film production continued as before. Compromise about film content was the order of the day and there was relatively little controversy between the Communist Party, the artists, and the audiences as to the proper role of the film in wartime. Most films therefore contained a "mix" of propaganda, art, and entertainment that suited all concerned. Only towards the end of the war did the readiness to compromise diminish once more——but a showdown was averted until after the war was over.

Political Content

The film "Front" (1943) is based on a play written the previous year. The theme is the need for modern military thinking. Stalin, as Commander-in-Chief, realizes that the heroes of the 1917 Revolution and Civil War are no longer up-to-date in their grasp of strategy and tactics. Stalin therefore dismisses the "Old Bolshevik" general Gorlov and replaces him with the younger Red Army commander Ognyov, who is also a member of the Party but has a superior grasp of modern warfare.

The film "Kutuzov" (1943) describes the strategy of deliberate retreat so successfully used by this tsarist general to defeat Napoleon in 1812. The clear implication of this picture is that victory in war may be accomplished without winning a particular battle—be it Borodino or Smolensk.

In the film "Slave #217" (1944) the "evil nature" of all Germans is depicted through suffering of a Russian girl sent into slavery in Germany. The seemingly innocent German civilians are revealed as brutal sadists who despise the Russian people. At the end of the film, the Russian slave returns to her homeland, confronts a group of German soldiers captured by the Soviet army, and announces that "they are all guilty."

Artistic Content

Even during the war the artistic genius of the director Eisenstein was not dimmed. His film epic "Ivan the Terrible" (1944), an inspired biography of the Russian tsar, again revealed Eisenstein's great skill, imagination, and directing talent. The use of light and shadow, the long-shots and close-ups, the melodramatic characterization of the principal roles and the evocation of mood of intrigue against the background of medieval Russia made this a film classic.

Entertainment Content

Despite the great reliance on Hollywood to supply the Soviet audiences with amusing films, some entertaining Soviet productions also appeared during the war. An example is "Kashchei the Immortal" (1944), based on a folk tale. The theme is the triumph of good over evil. Kashchei kidnaps a Russian girl. Nikita, her man, attempts her rescue and an old man gives him a cap which will make him invisible. Nikita catches up with Kashchei by means of a magic carpet and learns the secret by which he is able to kill the "immortal" Kashchei. At the end the lovers are re-united.[15]

Equally entertaining was the film "Arshin the Peddler" (1945), based on a comedy written thirty years previously by an Azerbaidzhan playwright. This film tells how a wealthy young man resorts to a disguise in order to woo his love. Her father, who disapproves of the young man, fails to recognize him and everything ends happily.

1946-1952

The atmosphere of compromise was shattered in 1946 when the Central Committee of the Communist Party banned four major Soviet films in a dramatic decree which was given considerable publicity. Among the victims were such outstanding artists as the directors Eisenstein and Pudovkin. The decree was concerned chiefly with the film "Great Life" (directed by Lukov) and criticized this picture in great detail. More important, however, was the warning (contained in the decree) that the Soviet film industry would have to undergo a severe reform with respect to film content. Both film artists and administrators—particularly the film industry chief, Bolshakov—were warned to mend their ways. The decree signalled the emergence of more severe political demands by the

---

[15]Film Chronicle, April 1944, pp. 3-8.

Communist Party, but neither the artists nor the audiences were prepared to surrender. The result was a drastic decline in production, followed by a decline in attendance wherever Soviet films were exhibited.[16]

Only a few films were produced from 1947 to 1952. The Communist Party took the position that quality was more important than quantity; consequently the urgent demand for more propaganda was maintained until Stalin's death. Two themes in particular were required: The Communist Party had to be depicted as the guiding force in all activities, and Stalin had to be personally involved in all decisions of any consequence. Thus the image of the benevolent and wise Communist official appeared in a great number of films and Stalin, too, played a role in many pictures.

Film artists resisted the new party line from its inception. Within a year of the publication of the decree "About the film 'Great Life,'" production of new films declined to the lowest point since 1933—and remained low for six years. More films were released during the single year 1928 than in the entire six-year period 1947-1952. The few films that were produced underwent numerous changes as film artists resisted the new policy at every step. The time required to produce a film increased tremendously. Many experienced directors released either one film during the period, or no films at all. Even fewer films were released by newcomers to the industry. The shortage of new films was matched by a shortage of new scenarios, as writers found other ways of spending their time. The artists were clearly dissatisfied and found numerous ways of expressing this dissatisfaction without resorting to

---

[16]Kul'tura i zhian' (Culture and Life), Moscow, June 30, 1948.

direct criticism of party policies. The film (as well as other arts)
was nearly paralyzed by the "inner emigration" of the artist.

The film audiences expressed their dissatisfaction at the box office.
While long lines formed outside the theaters to buy tickets to see the
Hollywood film "Tarzan," and other entertaining foreign pictures, the
Soviet press published complaints that movie theaters showing the latest
Soviet productions were not well attended. In view of the shortage of
new Soviet films, the exhibitors resorted to the practice of reviving
old films, or showing the same film in nearly all theaters at the same
time—but people found other things to do, and exhibition, like production, suffered until the end of the Stalin era. Despite the stiffening
of the Party line, some compromises were made here and there so that the
film industry survived. Although many films were banned, a few of these
were shown for short periods of time before being removed from the screen
because of "ideological defects." Even those productions which received
unqualified approval from the Party contained some elements of art and
entertainment.

Political Content

"The Battle of Stalingrad" (1949) depicted the brilliance of Stalin's
military strategy in great detail. The film was so long that it was produced and released in two separate parts, each as long as a full length
picture. The film begins with Stalin mapping his strategy, and eventually
shows Stalin dictating surrender terms (which were rejected by Hitler)
after the German armed forces in the Stalingrad area had been surrounded
and cut off. At the very end Stalin orders the destruction of the trapped
German forces. This picture was one of a series depicting Stalin's

military genius throughout the war. All these pictures attempted to create a distinctive art form--a film chronicle of significant historical events during World War II. The pseudo-documentary quality of these films constituted a new departure in Soviet film art insofar as they attempted to portray pseudo-historic events simultaneously from the point of view of the average soldier and the Commander-in-Chief.

Another propagandistic film was "Miners of the Don" (1951)--a treatment of the problem of technological unemployment and its solution in the Soviet Union. The solution depicted in the film is quite simple: the manual laborer goes back to school so that he may learn how to use modern machinery. The film depicts Stalin as an optimistic economic planner with a brilliant grasp of technology and industrial relations. On the artistic side, the film combines the facts of economic life with imaginative fantasy that makes a Soviet coal mine appear to be a most glamorous futuristic enterprise--with neon lights, high speed trains and fabulous tools and instruments. This "science fiction" treatment may have seemed real to those who have never seen a coal mine, but the producers of the film must be credited with great imagination.

Artistic Content

In addition to the new, dramatic pseudo-documentary genre mentioned above, some films produced during 1946-1952 contained artistic innovations of different kinds. The picture "Stone Flower" (1946) had some unusually dazzling color effects (by Soviet standards) but the credit probably goes to Germany rather than the Soviet Union because the picture was made with a new type of color emulsion developed in Germany; supplies of raw film stock of this new type were captured by the Soviet army at the end of the war. In any event, the colors were dazzling and brilliant, and therefore most appropriate to this entertaining fairy tale about "The Lady of the Copper Mountain" (1946) who guarded a treasure house of precious minerals and jewels.[17]

Another innovation was a series of musical biographies of Russian composers such as "Musorgski" (1950)--accounts of the lives of outstanding Russian composers interspersed with many scenes from their operas (photographed at the opera). "Musorgski," for instance, contains many scenes from his opera Boris Godunov. A number of other films dealt with the lives of poets, as for instance, "Taras Shevchenko" (1951). These films about artists not only described the problems inherent in the life of an artist, but also stressed the role of art in society. Although such pictures were not devoid of political propaganda, they were made with great care and attention to detail and managed to convey the struggles of artistic creation.

Entertainment Content

Not many films made during 1946-1952 could rank with "Stone Flower" (mentioned above) as sheer entertainment, but a few musical comedies were released during the period. Typical of this type was the film "Spring" (1947). This film had two themes: a secluded life is foolish, and people should "enjoy love while they can." The cast included a newspaper reporter, a movie director, an actress and a woman scientist; the scientist learns from the others that she should come out of her laboratory

---

[17]Manvell, R., Film, London, 1950, p. 201. See also Atkinson, O., Over at Uncle Joe's, New York, Bobbs-Merrill, 1947, p. 139.

once in a while to enjoy singing and dancing with other people. At the end of the film she realizes that "love is the spring season in human life."

The Dramatic Results of Successful Compromise: The Film "Chapayev" (1934)

The Soviet film industry continues to produce motion pictures and exhibit these to the public only because of a continuing process of compromise between the Communist Party, the artists and the audiences. The compromises are necessary for two reasons: each of the three groups has the power to destroy the film industry, and each group has its own definitions of the role of motion pictures in Soviet society. Thus, conflict is inevitable and compromise is indispensable. The Soviet film industry cannot operate successfully on any other basis.

The degree to which successful compromises can be achieved determines the fate not only of the entire film industry, but also the fate of each motion picture. Conflict unresolved by compromise nearly resulted in the destruction of the Soviet film industry (as a going concern) on several occasions: a low point in productivity was reached in 1933, and again during the period 1947-1952. Unresolved conflicts repeatedly resulted in the failure of specific motion pictures; some films were banned, others were artistic failures, and others were condemned at the box office. Successful compromise, on the other hand, resulted in spurts of high productivity in Soviet studios (with a peak in 1928) and a tremendous sale of admissions (exceeding one billion annually around 1939-1940). Successful compromise also resulted in a number of films that pleased all concerned: the Party, the artist, and the audiences.

By way of illustration, the film "Chapayev" (1934) will be briefly considered. This motion picture ranks with the most successful Soviet films ever made and exhibited. It serves as a good example of successful compromise between the Party, the artist, and the audiences. Thus it reveals the possibilities inherent in the Soviet film industry.

The film "Chapayev" was based on a book of the same name published during the 1920's, written by Dmitri Furmanov. The author recounts his experiences as a political commissar sent by the Communist Party to advise a small band of armed peasants led by a shoemaker-turned-commander named Chapayev. The group of fighting men, who had armed themselves during the Civil War to protect their families and property from marauders, first accepted Chapayev as their leader and then accepted Furmanov as their commissar. Thus they became "Red partisans," although the peasants—including Chapayev—knew virtually nothing about the political significance of the Civil War. During the period that Furmanov served as commissar, Chapayev's "army" attempted to protect lives and property in their native region and engaged in battles against an anti-Communist military force. Towards the end of the Civil War, Furmanov was reassigned to other work by the Communist Party and Chapayev's "army" was eventually annihilated in a surprise attack. The film ends on a positive note, however, as a powerful military force routs the enemy and avenges Chapayev's death.

This film was released to the public in 1934, just one year after the Soviet film industry had reached a low point in film production. The year 1934 had been chosen to celebrate the fifteenth anniversary of the Soviet film industry (based on the fact that Lenin had signed a decree

nationalizing the industry in 1919) and it was decided to plan a big
celebration in Moscow, in honor of this event. The Party wanted to
select one film to hold up as a model for Soviet film-makers, and Stalin
personally selected "Chapayev" as the film. At the celebration, awards
were made to the Lenfilm studio (which had released the picture) and to
all persons connected with the production of "Chapayev." The film was
highly advertised and widely exhibited.

Within five years, more than fifty million tickets to "Chapayev"
had been sold in the Soviet Union.[18] One of the respondents interviewed
in the Harvard University survey mentioned that he had seen the film "at
least ten times" and one out of every seven respondents reported having
seen this film. A number of respondents mentioned that they particularly
liked the film "Chapayev"; one respondent called it "amusing"; another
said it was "true to life." A few respondents criticized the picture for
its propaganda content, stating that "Furmanov [the commissar] was really
not such a brain" or that "there were some exaggerations." The consensus,
however, is that this picture was very popular. It was still being shown
in the Soviet Union regularly some 25 years after the date of its release.

Concerning the propaganda aspects of the film, it has been pointed
out that the real Chapayev "was a deeply religious man who punished Red
Army soldiers for disrespect to the clergy and once roused a village
priest in the middle of the night to conduct prayers for victory. The
scenario completely omitted this side of his character."[19] Furthermore

_____

[18]_Soviet Films 1938-1939_, Moscow, 1939, p. 84.

[19]Babitsky, P., _Soviet Film Industry_, New York, 1955, p. 160.

Chapayev's anarchistic tendencies were deleted in favor of political naivete, as evidenced in this bit of dialogue:

> Peasant Spokesman (to Chapayev): "Are you for the Bolsheviks or the Communists?"
>
> Chapayev: "I'm for the International."
>
> (Later.) Furmanov (to Chapayev): "Are you for the Second International or the Third?"
>
> Chapayev: "Which one is the best?"
>
> Furmanov: "The Third."
>
> Chapayev: "Is that the one Lenin belongs to?"
>
> (Furmanov nods.)
>
> Chapayev: "All right. You can count me in."

From the artistic standpoint, "Chapayev" is a realistic film with very little use of symbolism, montage, or trick photography. The characters are not stereotyped, however; "Chapayev" is depicted as having a few common vices (he curses and throws furniture around) and the anti-Communist colonel is shown as a man of culture and refinement (constantly playing Beethoven's music on the piano and wearing white gloves wherever he goes). Thus, the film could scarcely be considered a great work of art, but it is a workmanlike production with occasional touches of real skill on the part of the producers and the cast.

In conclusion, the Soviet film "Chapayev" succeeded in pleasing its political sponsors (the Communist Party) and its financial sponsors (the Soviet audiences) as well as the many artists who worked on this film, and wrote numerous articles expressing their satisfaction with the production. Thus the Soviet motion picture industry, by means of compromise, was able to produce this picture to everyone's satisfaction. Pictures like "Chapayev" have kept the Soviet film industry going from 1918 to the present day.

PART V

SUMMARY OF CONCLUSIONS

CHAPTER X

SUMMARY OF CONCLUSIONS

The thesis presented here has interpreted the history of the Soviet
film in terms of the continuing accommodation of conflicting views on
the purposes of motion-pictures. It has been suggested that different
social roles and group memberships are conducive to different definitions
of the cinema's social role, and that these conflicting definitions are
regularly subject to compromise. The operation of the Soviet motion-
picture industry depends on continuing reconciliation of viewpoints
between three powerful groups: political leaders, artistic personnel,
and film audiences.

A review of published materials written by a number of social scientists, film historians, and critics revealed some broad areas of agreement concerning the basic dynamics of the Soviet film industry. Virtually
all of these published studies focused attention on one or two of the
three key groups (political authorities, creative artists, and film audiences) and documented the views and activities of these groups. Many of
the books and articles about Soviet films called attention to the interaction between these groups and related this interaction to film production and film content. A thorough study of these publications revealed,
however, that none of the interpretations focused on all three of the
key groups. It is this new focus which provides the basis for this dissertation and permits a more comprehensive understanding of the subject.

The present thesis stresses the power of all three groups—political authorities, artistic personnel, and film audiences—and their unique definitions of the primary purpose of the film. The political authorities continually demand propaganda. The artists insist on the right to make films according to their artistic inclinations and to use the motion-picture as a vehicle for self-expression. The audiences expect films to entertain them. Thus, each of the three groups makes specific demands on the motion-picture industry.

Each group has the power to disrupt motion-picture production. The political authorities have at their command police powers and funds, which can be used to strengthen or to weaken the film industry. The artists have the creative abilities and technical competence which are necessary to motion-picture production, and they are free to contribute or to withhold their abilities. The audiences exercise the right to attend or not to attend film showings; their presence or absence in movie theaters not only influences the financial strength of the industry, but also challenges the ultimate purpose of film production. which is exhibition, for the film industry would serve no useful purpose if audiences were lacking.

The differences in definition, combined with the power exercised by each of the three groups, has consistently led to an element of instability which could only be neutralized through compromise. The necessity for compromise is tacitly recognized by all three groups, insofar as each group has a vested interest in the viability of the film industry. A permanent compromise cannot be achieved because each new film gives rise to additional controversies and requires further compromise. Therefore,

each of the three groups finds itself chained to the "bargaining table,"
but too weak to dictate surrender terms to the others. Thus it is necessary for all concerned to "negotiate" continually with the other parties to the ever-present conflict.

Conflicting Definitions of the Film

Political Definitions

The political authorities in the Soviet Union define the function
of the film industry chiefly in terms of propaganda. Together with other
mass media of communication (such as the press, radio and television)
and the arts (such as the theater, music, literature, dance, circus and
so on), the motion-picture was defined as a medium for transmitting a
political doctrine from the political elite to the broad masses of the
population. This particular doctrine, which has been called "Marxism,"
"Leninism" and other names, was formulated and reformulated by the political leaders of the Communist regime in the Soviet Union and was generally
translated into specific terms by the Department for Agitation and
Propaganda of the Communist Party. Insofar as the political doctrine
pertained to all areas of human relations, such as morals, economic relationships and so on, it came very close to being a comprehensive "Welt-
anschauung"--a cosmic view of the universe. In this connection, Communist
leaders not only developed definite notions about film content, but also
artistic style. The style that won official approval came to be called
"socialist realism" and was defined by political authorities. Thus the
Communist Party evolved very specific definitions of film function, content and style. All these definitions were formulated to promote the

Communist ideology and to serve the needs of the Communist Party.

The political definition of the film had several subsidiary aspects relating to the principal concern with propaganda. Among these was the politically motivated desire to make films compete with the church and the alcoholic beverage industry, so as to weaken these two institutions; the Communist Party hoped to attract people to the movie theaters and thereby to empty the churches and taverns. Another function assigned to the motion-picture industry by the Communist Party was visual education on scientific, technical and military lines; to achieve this purpose, films were to be made so as to impart factual information to the general population. Furthermore, the Communist Party considered films to be works of art demonstrating the high level of "culture" in Soviet society; in this context the film was considered to be like the ballet and other artistic products of talent and genius. The political definition of films also considered the need for communication between the Soviet Union and other nations, so that the motion-picture was destined to serve as an ambassador abroad. The profit-making possibilities of the motion-picture industry were also recognized and Communist officials did not hesitate to ask that film exhibition yield funds to the Communist Party and the Soviet Government.

The multiplicity of aspects inherent in the total political definition of the Soviet film had some advantages and some disadvantages as far as the Communist Party was concerned. On the one hand, the various demands weakened the Party's bargaining position in its continuing "negotiations" with film industry artists and audiences simply because the complexity of the Communist position at the "bargaining table" made it difficult for the Party "negotiators" to translate all these demands into concrete terms with respect to a particular film and scenes within that film. On the other hand, the variety of aspects inherent in the Communist definition always made it possible for Communist "negotiators" to achieve some gains, at least, because a compromise might satisfy one political requirement even though it failed to satisfy others. Thus there was considerable flexibility in the Communist position, and this flexibility permitted the Party to compromise continuously in the "bargaining" process without losing "face" and without detracting from the powerful position of the political authorities.

Artistic Definitions

Although the artistic personnel of the Soviet film industry generally defined the functions of the motion-picture in terms similar to those developed by political leaders, the artists usually disagreed with the politicians as to the relative importance of propaganda on the one hand and art on the other. To the artists, propaganda was more or less important, depending on the individual artist's own political outlook—but virtually all artists agreed that the film, being a work of art, ought to express the artist's creativity first of all. Thus the actors, writers and directors of the film industry defined the purpose of the motion-picture mainly in terms of artistic expression and concerned themselves primarily with individual style and approach. Consequently, the artists found themselves at odds with the politicians (and audiences) with regard to the basic definition of the function of films in Soviet society. Nevertheless the artists recognized and understood other definitions and usually were willing to compromise with the other groups, provided that the importance of the artist's role was not overlooked. Being indispensable to the production of motion-pictures, the artist was usually able to win some concessions, particularly because politicians and audiences both tacitly recognized the importance of artistic creativity in the genesis of motion-pictures.

Audience Definitions

Film audiences in the Soviet Union defined the motion-picture chiefly as an entertainment medium. While movie-goers sometimes expected films to explain political affairs or to confront the spectator with an inspiring work of art, members of the huge film audience generally agreed that motion-pictures ought to be entertaining first of all. While entertainment was by no means limited to a particular genre, such as comedy or melodrama, audience appreciation hinged principally on the evaluation of each film's ability to entertain. Pictures that were judged "too political" (or "too symbolic") did not fare well at the box office, but some films criticized by the Party for insufficient propaganda content enjoyed considerable success because of their entertainment qualities; some diverting foreign films, many of them politically innocent, also proved very successful with Soviet audiences whenever they were shown. Some spectators undoubtedly tried to see all the films, but others were more selective and often succeeded in learning about the film in advance so that they could decide whether or not to spend time and money at the movie theater. Therefore the box office receipts generally reflected the opinions of the potential audience, not merely the actual audience for each film. Political leaders and film industry personnel generally studied box office statistics to ascertain audience reaction.

Power Relationships in the Soviet Film Industry

The Power of the Party

A few students of Soviet affairs have maintained that Communist
power is superficial and unstable, but the majority view appears to be
that the Communist Party is well entrenched in the Soviet Union, to say
the least, and controls every sphere of activity without question. This
majority view pervades published studies about the Soviet motion-picture
industry. Many books and articles about Soviet films mentioned some instances when the power of the Party was successfully challenged, but these
episodes were generally dismissed as being without significance. This
apparent contradiction between fact and conclusion demanded further study,
however.

In this dissertation an attempt was made to <u>measure</u> the power of the
Communist Party over the film industry. The analysis revealed fluctuations in the average propaganda content of Soviet films at various time
periods. These fluctuations were related to the limitations on the power
of the Communist Party. This interpretation resolved the apparent contradiction noted in earlier studies.

The power of the Communist Party in Soviet film affairs can best be
understood by considering it together with the power of film artists and
audiences. In this context it appears that the Party lacks absolute control just because the other two groups exercise some control over films
as well. Consequently the power of the Party is limited, although by no
means inconsiderable. Thus the Party has jailed film artists but has
never been able to "create" good films. Similarly, the Party has banned
entertaining pictures but has not coerced audiences into the movie

theaters to watch "politically acceptable" films. The occasional use of excessive Communist Party power has invariably resulted in resistance by artists and audiences, with the result that film production and attendance declined. This "action-reaction" manifested itself not only in the case of particular films, but also during several time periods between 1918 and 1952.

An effort was made in this dissertation to measure the relation between the propaganda content of films (reflecting the exercise of power by the Communist Party) and the volume of film production. By means of a content analysis that measured three elements of propaganda—time periods depicted in films, Communist affiliation of the hero, and the ideological characteristics of the plot—it was demonstrated that the propaganda content of Soviet films fluctuated at various times. The propaganda content was relatively more pronounced during the period 1929-1933, and again during the period 1946-1952; on the other hand there was relatively less propaganda during the period 1923-1928 and the period 1941-1945. A composite index, based on all three of the propaganda elements measured in the content analysis, confirmed the impression that the degree of propaganda content fluctuated inversely with the volume of motion-picture production. Thus propaganda content reached its peaks about the same time that film production fell off. This finding tends to confirm the thesis that the power of the Communist Party is by no means unchallenged in the motion-picture industry.

The Power of the Artists

Without exception, previously published works on the subject of the Soviet film disregarded the power of the artists. While some consideration was given to their views about film art, the artist's motivation was generally overlooked; a few students of the Soviet film industry noted the attractive material incentives, and probably assumed that such material incentives were sufficient to motivate Soviet artists to the utmost. It must be pointed out that the film director Eisenstein was usually considered to be in a class by himself—a temperamental artistic genius dedicated to theory and experiment—but his passion was generally dismissed as eccentric.

It would be more correct to consider Eisenstein an extreme case of a personality structure common to most talented artists—and there were many such persons working in the Soviet film industry during the period 1918-1952. These artists were motivated by an intense desire for self-expression, and their creativity was more easily stifled by administrative interference than by the absence of material incentives. The curtailment of artistic freedom, whether by government decree or by audience indifference, led to severe disturbances in motion-picture production. Writers, actors and directors expected to be given a free hand to experiment and to create works of art, and they resisted efforts to curtail their artistic freedom. This resistance was manifested not only by a loss of interest in the work (and the consequent decline of their creativity) but also—in some cases—by total withdrawal from the motion-picture industry. This protest was an important factor in the dramatic decline of Soviet film production on several occasions.

The power of artists stemmed from the fact that they were largely irreplaceable. The profession of film artists requires not only an unusual degree of talent but also a long period of training and experience in film work. Such personnel could not be easily replaced. Thus the

artist had it within his power to refuse his services, thereby bringing
about a significant decline in the productivity of the motion-picture
industry.

By means of statistics pertaining to the number of film directors
in the industry from 1918 to 1952, it was demonstrated that "shortages"
of experienced and active artists could only be attributed to their un-
willingness to work, since the actual number of such persons available
to the Soviet motion-picture industry often exceeded the number of work
assignments in film studios (as measured by the number of films released
each year). Thus it became apparent that declines in productivity reflected a lack of motivation rather than a shortage of experienced
artists. The statistical evidence was confirmed by statements published
in the Soviet press after Stalin's death and may be summarized in this
quotation from the Soviet newspaper Literaturnaya gazeta: "How is it
possible to disregard the creative aspirations of the artists? For the
prolonged silence of our leading directors the system itself is chiefly
to blame."[1]

The Power of the Audiences

Although Soviet films were exported abroad from time to time, the
principal audience for Soviet pictures was always the movie-going seg-
ment of the domestic population. This Soviet audience expanded rapidly
during the 1920's and 1930's, and was buying more than a billion movie
tickets annually by 1940. The Soviet film audience, which was composed
to a large extent of young, urban "middle class" people, continued to
have a considerable growth potential; both the Party and film industry
artists hoped for the further expansion of this audience. At the same

----

[1]Literaturnaya gazeta, Moscow, July 1, 1954.

time politicians and artists realized that film-goers were not irrevo-
cably committed; the audiences could choose to go or not to go to the
movies. Therefore, audience preferences were ascertained on the basis
of box office returns for each individual film, and also by careful study
of "fan" mail, attitude surveys, and comments solicited at previews.

Box office statistics were seldom published, however. Books and
articles published in the Soviet Union had virtually nothing to say
about audience preferences. Once in a great while an article in the
Soviet press would allude to the success or failure of a film at the
box office, but statements of this kind were rare indeed. Foreign observers sometimes attempted to fill the void by publishing their impressions of audience preferences, but these estimates were usually based on
scanty evidence. Nevertheless, most foreign observers apparently agreed
that entertaining films based on music or romance were always popular
with Soviet audiences, whereas propaganda-laden films did not always
appeal successfully to the potential audience.

Soviet film production and exhibition policies also suggested the
strength of the popular desire for entertainment. A number of politically innocent films were released by Soviet studios nearly every year,
and similar films were imported for exhibition in the Soviet Union.
Since many of the foreign films contained little or no propaganda, it is
reasonable to conclude that their exhibition was intended to satisfy the
audience demand for non-political entertainment.

A team of American social scientists, who interviewed former Soviet
citizens to learn about daily life in the U.S.S.R., ascertained that
some Soviet citizens went to the movies quite often—once a week or

more (around 1940). The interviewers also learned that some of the film-goers accepted Soviet pictures without reservations, while others carefully selected films to see; pictures were usually selected if they promised to be entertaining, and contained only a modicum of propaganda. Analysis of the list of film titles recalled by the respondents (in reply to the question: "Which films do you recall having seen in the Soviet Union?") revealed that the propaganda content of the films recalled was not essentially different from that of all Soviet motion-pictures produced about that time (1934-1940). This finding reflected the results of compromise in the Soviet motion-picture industry: film audiences had become reconciled to some political content in films, provided that this propaganda was confined to an acceptable level.

The Process of Compromise

The production of a feature film generally required a year or more. At each stage of the production process, from the preparation of the first outline to the final preview, there were numerous opportunities to change the content of the proposed film. (Several people who personally participated in the production of Soviet films reported that changes were commonplace.) The completed film frequently bore little resemblance to the initial scenario outline.

Within the studio, many forces were at work. Representatives of the Communist Party were present at all administrative and operating levels. Writers, directors and actors involved in film production had many opportunities to make (or influence) decisions about film content. Although film audiences were not directly represented, their views were

solicited from time to time in various ways: proposed scenarios were
occasionally published in advance of filming, motion-pictures were shown
to "test audiences" prior to the official release of these pictures,
and so on. In addition, administrators had box office figures to guide
them, together with more detailed audience comments addressed to newspaper editors and to the film studios.

The compromises made in the course of film production were supplemented by exchanges of views at studio conferences, in the press and at
nationwide meetings where Soviet films were regularly discussed. All
personnel connected with film studios were periodically summoned to attend discussions of recently produced pictures, and similar meetings
were convened on a nationwide basis from time to time under the sponsorship of the Communist Party and the governmental motion-picture administration. A number of publications were devoted exclusively to motion-
picture affairs and contained articles written by Party officials, administrators, artists and critics. In addition, ordinary newspapers and
magazines occasionally printed film reviews or discussions of trends in
the film industry. Furthermore, a number of "film appreciation" groups
existed in the Soviet Union and sponsored the exchange of views through
meetings and publications. Thus, general discussions of film industry
developments took place frequently, and supplemented the detailed exchanges of views which occurred in the course of film production.

Film Content and Film Production

Virtually all completed films released by Soviet studios between
1918 and 1952 contained some elements of politics, art and entertainment.
The "mix" of these three elements varied from film to film, and from

time to time, but the basic ingredients were always present to some extent. Even during those periods (1929-1933 and 1946-1952) when political pressure increased considerably, Soviet film studios continued to produce and release some pictures that contained a high degree of artistry and entertainment. At no time was the production of films limited exclusively to mere propaganda, although there was a tendency in this direction during the periods when political pressure was greatest. These relatively intense political demands had other consequences, however; the volume of film production declined, as did attendance.

Thus, the artists and audiences reacted to increased political pressure in two ways: they stubbornly demanded the production of some artistic and entertaining films despite the Party's demand for more propaganda; they withdrew their support in connection with the production and exhibition of those pictures which they considered excessively political, or insufficiently artistic and entertaining. The combined power of the artists and audiences was so impressive that the Communist Party had to retreat. The political demand for propaganda was modified until artists and audiences again gave their support to the motion-picture industry.

Virtually all Soviet films contained some elements of propaganda, art and entertainment, and the majority balanced these three elements of content in such a way as to satisfy the political authorities, artists and audiences. Occasionally a film achieved a perfect balance of these elements and became a tremendous success. Whenever the elements of the "mix" were harmoniously combined, a film was sure to receive lavish praise from the Party and the critics, and to reap tremendous profits at the box office. Film audiences gladly went to see such films again and again, and these pictures were exhibited for decades. Successful films were frequently exported as well, and netted profits and praise abroad. As for the artists who created such pictures, they received many honors and ample rewards from the government, along with immense satisfaction for a job well done.

Thus, conflicts were inevitable, because of different definitions of the role of the film in Soviet society, but successful compromises made it possible to produce some films that satisfied everyone and thereby revitalized the Soviet film industry.

BIBLIOGRAPHY

"About Young Cadres of Screen Directors and Scenario Writers," Literatur-naya gazeta, November 24, 1951, pp. 3-4. Translated in Current Digest of the Soviet Press, Volume III, Number 47, pp. 5-7.

Abbot, Jere, "Notes on the Movies," Hound and Horn, Volume II, Number 2, January/March 1929, pp. 159-62.

Adlow, Dorothy, "Soviet Cinema: A Thriving Art," The Christian Science Monitor, October 24, 1934, Magazine Section, pp. 8-9.

Albig, William, Public Opinion, New York, McGraw-Hill, 1939.

Aleksandrov, G. F., "Rech" (Speech [to the Council of Nationalities]), Sovetskaya kultura, April 29, 1954, p. 2.

Alexandrov, G. V., S. Eisenstein, and V. Pudovkin, "The Sound Film: A Statement from the USSR," Close Up, October 1928, pp. 10-13.

"Ambassador," Time, Volume 43, June 12, 1944, p. 54.

Anderson, Joseph L., "Soviet Films Since 1945," Films in Review, New York, National Board of Review of Motion Pictures, Inc., Volume IV, Number 1, January 1953, pp. 7-14, and Number 2, February 1953, pp. 64-73.

Anstrey, E., "Day in Soviet Russia," Spectator, Volume 167, August 22, 1941, p. 179.

_____, "Leningrad Fights," Spectator, Volume 169, Number 13, 1942, p. 455.

Arakelyan, A., Upravleniye sotsialisticheskoi promyshlennostyu (Adminis-tration of Socialist Industry), Moscow, Moscow Worker [Press], 1947.

Arnheim, Rudolf, Film, London, Faber and Faber, 1933.

Arsharuni, A., "The Cinema of the Central Asia Republics of the USSR," in Soviet Cinema, edited by A. Arosev, Moscow, VOKS, 1935, pp. 143-44.

Atkinson, O., Over at Uncle Joe's, New York, Bobbs-Merrill, 1947.

Attasheva, Pearl, "The Talking Cinema in the USSR," Close Up, September 1929, pp. 209-11.

_____, "News of the Soviet Cinema," Close Up, October 1929, pp. 309-18, and September 1930, pp. 177-83.

Atzizian, B., "A Few Words on Soviet Armenia's Cinematography," in *Soviet Cinema*, edited by A. Arosev, Moscow, VOKS, 1935, pp. 141-42.

Babitsky, Paul, and Martin Lutich, *The Soviet Movie Industry: Two Studies*, New York, Research Program on the USSR, Mimeographed Series Number 31, 1953.

_____, and John Rimberg, *The Soviet Film Industry*, New York, Frederick A. Praeger, 1955.

Babochkin, B., "How I Worked on 'Chapayev,'" in *Soviet Cinema*, edited by A. Arosev, Moscow; VOKS, 1935, pp. 157-61.

Bajan, M., "Dovzhenko: Soviet Cinema Director," *New Theatre*, April 1934, p. 6.

Bakshy, Alexander, "Russian Contribution," *Nation*, Volume 127, July 25, 1928, pp. 94-96.

Balkoff-Drowne, Tatiana, "Sadko," *Films in Review*, Volume IV, Number 7, August/September 1953, pp. 361-62.

Barbusse, Henri, *One Looks at Russia*, London, J. M. Dent and Sons, 1931.

Bardeche, Maurice, and Robert Brasillach, *History of Motion Pictures*, translated and edited by Iris Barry, New York, W. W. Norton, Inc., 1938.

Barr, Alfred H., Jr., "The Researches of Eisenstein," *Drawing and Design*, June 1928, pp. 155-56.

_____, "Sergei Michailovitch Eisenstein," *The Arts*, Volume XIV, Number 6, December 1928, pp. 316-21.

"Battle for the Ukraine," *Spectator*, Volume 172, April 7, 1944, p. 311.

"Battleship Potemkin," *New Statesman*, Volume 34, November 16, 1929, p. 191.

Beiswanger, G., "Soviet Russia at War," *Theatre Arts*, Volume 26, November 1942, pp. 682-89.

Belfrage, Cedric, "Russia's 'Gollywood,'" *World Film News*, September 1936, pp. 16-17.

Birukova, Vera, *National Film Studios in the USSR*, Moscow, VOKS, 1945.

Bishop, Christopher, "An Interview with Buster Keaton," *Film Quarterly*, Berkeley, University of California Press, Volume XII, Number 1, Fall 1958, pp. 15-22.

Bissonnette, George, Moscow Was My Parish, New York, McGraw-Hill, 1956.

Blakeston, Orwell, "Three Russian Films," Close Up, August 1929, pp. 144-50.

Bol'shakov, Ivan, "Stalin Prizes for Cinema," Information Bulletin, Washington, Embassy of the USSR, February 16, 1946, p. 152.

_____, "Tridtsat' let' sovetskogo kino" (Thirty Years of the Soviet Movies), 30 let sovetskoi kinematografii (30 Years of Soviet Cinematography) edited by D. Yeremin, Moscow, Goskinoizdat, 1950, pp. 5-27.

_____, "Vital Tasks of Cinematography," Pravda, September 14, 1951, p. 2. Translated in Current Digest of the Soviet Press, Volume III, Number 36, pp. 10-11.

Bond, R., "Dovzhenko on the Sound Film," Close Up, October 1930, pp. 273-75.

Britton, Lionel, "Kino Eye: Vertov and the Newest Film Spirit of Russia," The Realist, October 1929, pp. 126-38.

Bryher, Winifred, Film Problems of Soviet Russia, Riant Chateau, Territet [Switzerland], Pool, 1929.

Burov, Semyon, "Realism the Basis of Soviet Film Art," Film Review, London, Penguin, Number 4, October 1947.

Carter, Huntly, The New Theatre and Cinema of Soviet Russia, London, Chapman and Dodd, 1924.

_____, The New Spirit in the Russian Theatre, 1917-28 (and a sketch of the Russian Kinema and Radio 1919-22, Showing the new Communal Relationship between the Three), London, Brentano's, 1929.

_____, "The Soviet Cinema and the People: Their Social Unity," Playtime in Russia, edited by Hubert Griffith, London, Methuen, 1935.

Cinema Chronicle. See Film Chronicle.

"Cinema: Current Trends in Soviet Production," Spectator, Volume 174, March 16, 1945, p. 243.

"Cinema in Europe," Living Age, Volume 357, November 1939, pp. 272-76.

"Cinema Industry in the USSR, The," Soviet Union Review, Washington, D. C., April 1929, pp. 63-65.

Cole, Lester, "Unhappy Ending," Hollywood Quarterly, October 1945, pp. 80-84.

Collegium of USSR Ministry of Cinematography, "About Young Cadres of Screen Directors and Scenario Writers," Literaturnaya gazeta, November 24, 1951, p. 2. Translated in Current Digest of the Soviet Press, Volume III, Number 47, January 5, 1952, p. 8.

Counts, George S. and Nucia Lodge, The Country of the Blind, Boston, Houghton Mifflin, 1949.

"Cultural Influence of the Cinema," School and Society, Volume 50, September 9, 1939, p. 340.

Dana, Henry W. L., Handbook on Soviet Drama, New York, American-Russian Institute, 1938.

"Defeat of the Germans Before Moscow," New Statesman & Nation, Volume 23, June 27, 1942, p. 420.

"Development of the Cinema Activity in the USSR," International Review of Educational Cinematography, March 1932, p. 218.

de la Roche, Catherine, "Soviet Cinema," Spectator, Volume 175, July 6, 1945, p. 7.

_____, "Scenic Design in the Soviet Cinema," Film Review, London, Penguin Books, Number 3, August 1947.

_____, "Soviet Cinema and Youth," Film Review, London, Penguin Books, Number 4, October 1947.

_____, "Soviet Cinema and Science," Film Review, London, Penguin Books, Number 5, January 1948.

_____, and Thorold Dickinson, Soviet Cinema, London, Falcon Press, 1948.

Dickinson, Thorold and Alan Lawson, "The Film in the USSR--1937," Cine-Technician, London, Association of Cine-Technicians, August/September 1937, pp. 95-111.

Dickinson, Thorold, "Marie Seton: Eisenstein," Soviet Studies, Volume V, pp. 167-76.

_____, "Some Aspects of Soviet Film-Making," Geographical Magazine, London, Volume XXVII, Number 2, June 1954, pp. 95-106.

Dieterle, William, "Reflections on Soviet Pictures," Soviet Russia Today, December 1937, pp. 8-10.

Dinamov, Sergei, "Art of the Soviet Cinema," International Literature, Moscow, February 1935, pp. 64-74.

_____, "Film Art in White Russia," in Soviet Cinema, edited by A. Arosev, Moscow, VOKS, 1935, pp. 111-22.

Doolittle, Hilda, "Russian Films," Close Up, September 1928, pp. 18-32.

Dreiser, Theodore, Dreiser Looks at Russia, New York, Horace Liveright, 1928.

Eastman, Fred, "Motion Pictures in Russia," Christian Century, Volume 53, September 9, 1936, pp. 1185-87.

Eastman, Max, Artists in Uniform, New York, Knopf, 1934.

Eisenstein, Sergei M., "Mass Movies," Nation, Volume 125, November 9, 1927, pp. 507-08.

_____, "Filming Art and Training," Close Up, March 1930, pp. 195-97.

_____, "Mexican Film and Marxian Theory: Reply to E. Wilson," New Republic, Volume 69, December 9, 1931, pp. 99-100.

_____, "Detective Work in the G.I.K.," Close Up, December 1932, pp. 287-94.

_____, "Cinematography with Tears," Close Up, March 1933, pp. 3-17.

_____, "An American Tragedy," Close Up, June 1933, pp. 109-24.

_____, "Autobiography," International Literature, October 1933, pp. 128-29.

_____, "Through Theatre to Cinema," Theatre Arts, Volume 20, September 1936, pp. 735-47.

_____, "The Mistakes of 'Eezhin Lug'," International Literature, Moscow, August 1937, Number 8, pp. 97-99.

_____, "Montage in 1938," Life and Letters Today, Volume 21, June 1939, pp. 93-101.

_____, The Soviet Screen, Moscow, Foreign Languages Publishing House, 1939.

_____, "The Cinema," in USSR Speaks for Itself, London, Lawrence and Wishart, 1941.

_____, and V. Pudovkin, "There is Rage in Russia," World Film News, September 1937, p. 5.

"Eisenstein's Plans," Living Age, Volume 342, July 1932, pp. 462-63.

Ellis, Peter and Jay Leyda, "A Guide to the Social Study of the Film," Theatre Workshop, April/July 1937, pp. 73-79.

"End of St. Petersburg," New Republic, Volume 55, June 13, 1928, pp. 97-98.

Erikson, Erik H., "The Legend of Maxim Gorky's Youth," in Childhood and Society, New York, W. W. Norton, 1950, pp. 316-58.

Ermler, F., "The Films," International Literature, May 1935, pp. 118-19.

Evans, Ernestine, "The Soviet Idea in the 'Kino,'" Asia, New York, Asia, August 1926, pp. 698-701.

_____, "Armored Cruiser, Prince Potemkin," Nation, Volume 123, September 15, 1926, p. 252.

Farber, M., "Russian Victory," New Republic, Volume 109, October 11, 1943, p. 487.

Fearing, Franklin, "Influence of the Movies on Attitudes and Behavior," Annals of the American Academy of Political and Social Science, November 1947, pp. 70-79.

Feldman, K., "The Reconstruction of the Soviet Cinema," V.O.K.S., Volume II, Numbers 10-12, 1931, pp. 56-66.

"Fifteen Years of Soviet Cinema," International Literature, January 1935, pp. 104-05.

"Fifteen Years of the Soviet Cinema," Economic Review of the Soviet Union, January 1935, pp. 8-9.

Film Chronicle (also called Soviet Film Chronicle, Cinema Chronicle, and Soviet Cinema), Moscow, VOKS, 1943-1946. Mimeographed.

"Film in Moscow," Spectator, Volume 147, October 31, 1931, pp. 565-66.

"Film in Soviet Russia," Great Britain and the East, Volume 49, September 16, 1937, p. 395.

"Films Abroad," Living Age, Volume 350, July 1936, pp. 441-43.

Fischer, Louis, Soviet Journey, New York, Smith and Haas, 1935.

Florinsky, Michael T., Toward an Understanding of the USSR, New York, Macmillan, 1939.

Ford, Charles, "Russian Films Before the Soviets," Films in Review, Volume IV, Number 9, November 1953, pp. 472-74.

_____, "Moscow Goes to the Movies," Sight & Sound, London, British Film Institute, Volume IV, Number 21, Spring 1937, pp. 9-11.

Freeman, Joseph, and others, Voices of October; Art and Literature in Soviet Russia, New York, Vanguard Press, 1930.

Freeman, Joseph, _An American Testament_, New York, Farrar and Rinehart, 1936.

Gerstein, Evelyn, "Potemkin," _New Republic_, Volume 48, October 20, 1926, pp. 243-44.

_____, "Russia's Film Wizard: A Study of the Career and Achievements of Eisenstein," _Theatre Guild Magazine_, February 1930, p. 44.

Geyer, O. R., "Winning Foreign Film Markets," _Scientific American_, Volume 125, August 20, 1921, p. 132.

Giese, Hans-Joachim, _Die Film-Wochenschau in Dienste der Politik_, Dresden, M. Dittert, 1940.

Golden, Nathan D., _Motion Picture Markets, 1944_, Inquiry Reference Service, U. S. Department of Commerce, 1944.

Grierson, John, "The Russian Cineman Bear Awakens: The Movie Situation in the Land of the Muscovites," _Motion Picture Classic_, June 1927, pp. 18-19.

Grinko, G. T., _The Five-Year Plan of the Soviet Union_, New York, International Publishers, 1931.

Groshev, A., "For the Further Development of Soviet Cinematography," _Kommunist_, Moscow, July 1955, pp. 50-61. Condensed and translated in _Current Digest of the Soviet Press_, Volume VII, Number 31, pp. 10-12.

Gorshkov, V., "Molodezh' strany sotsializma' (Youth of the Land of Socialism), in _Molodezh' sovetskogo kino_ (Youth of the Soviet Movies), Moscow, Goskinoizdat, 1938, pp. 2-9.

Harley, John Eugene, _World-Wide Influences of the Cinema_, Los Angeles, University of Southern California Press, 1940.

Harper, Samuel Northrup, _Civic Training in Soviet Russia_, Chicago, University of Chicago Press, 1929.

Harper, Samuel Northrup and R. Thompson, _The Government of the Soviet Union_, New York, Van Nostrand, 1949. Second edition.

Hellmund-Waldow, E., "The Russian Film Industry," _Close Up_, Volume II, Number 5, May 1928, pp. 65-70.

Hibben, Paxton, "Movies in Russia," _Nation_, Volume 121, November 11, 1925, pp. 539-40.

Higgins, Marguerite, _Red Plush and Black Bread_, New York, Doubleday, 1955.

Hope, Bob, "I Found the Russians Can Laugh Too," Look, Des Moines, Volume 22, Number 12, June 10, 1958, pp. 27-30.

"How They Control Movies Abroad," Literary Digest, Volume 114, August 6, 1932, p. 22.

Hughes, Langston, I Wonder as I Wander: An Autobiographical Journey, New York, Rinehart, 1956.

Hunter, William, Scrutiny of Cinema, London, Wishart, 1932.

Huth, Arno, Freedom to Listen, United Nations Economic and Social Council, Commission on Human Rights, Sub-Commission on Freedom of Information and of the Press, October 2, 1951. (51-16721. E/CN.4/ Sub. 1/155).

Ilyinsky, Igor, "Serious Remarks about the Comical," Literaturnaya gazeta, September 18, 1951, p. 3. Translated in Current Digest of the Soviet Press, Volume III, Number 39, p. 10.

Ingster, Boris, "Serge Eisenstein," Hollywood Quarterly, Volume V, Summer 1951, pp. 380-88.

Inkeles, Alex, Public Opinion in Soviet Russia: A Study in Mass Persuasion, Cambridge, Harvard University Press, 1950.

"Ivan the Progressive," Nation, Volume 163, July 20, 1946, p. 60.

Johnston, Winifred, Memo on the Movies: War Propaganda 1914-1939, Norman, Oklahoma, Cooperative Books, Series I, Number 5, 1939.

Kalashnikov, Yu. and G. Mdivani, "Important Questions on Film Production," Kul'tura i zhizn', January 11, 1951, p. 3. Translated in Current Digest of the Soviet Press, Volume III, Number 1, pp. 14-15.

Katayev, V. and A. Macheret, "Soviet Cinema," U.S.S.R. in Construction, January 1938, pp. 1-25.

Katsman, R., "Peredovye zhurnalisty ekrana" (Traveling Journalists of the Screen), in Molodezh' sovetskogo kino (Youth of the Soviet Movies), edited by Semyon L. Ginzburg, Moscow, Goskinoizdat, 1938, pp. 46-65.

Katsygras, A., "The Cinema in the Collective Farms," in Soviet Cinema, edited by A. Arosev, Moscow, VOKS, 1935, pp. 217-20.

Klingender, F. D., "Reasons for Change of Style in Russian Films," World Film News, August 1936, p. 24.

Kopytov, A., "Kinoset' sovetskogo soyuza za tridtsat' let" (Movie Network of the Soviet Union After Thirty Years), in 30 let sovetskoi kinematografii (30 Years of Soviet Cinematography), edited by D. Yeremin, Moscow, Goskinoizadat, 1950, pp. 152-61.

Kotiev, B., "Popularization of the Cinema in the USSR," in Soviet Cinema, edited by A. Arosev, Moscow, VOKS, 1935, pp. 213-16.

Koval, Francis, "Venice 1953," Films in Review, Volume IV, Number 8, October 1953, pp. 385-93.

Kunitz, J., "Eisenstein's Resurgence," New Republic, Volume 98, March 29, 1939, pp. 222-23.

Lambert, Gavin, "Film Festival in San Francisco," Film Quarterly, Berkeley, University of California Press, Volume XII, Number 1, Fall 1958, pp. 24-25.

Lania, Leo, "A New Stage in the Development of the Soviet Film," Life and Letters Today, Summer 1936, pp. 161-66.

_____, "Films in Birth," Living Age, Volume 351, November 1936, pp. 251-53.

Lang, Daniel, "A Reporter at Large," New Yorker, Volume 27, Number 53, February 16, 1952, pp. 67-81.

Lasswell, Harold D., "The Scope of Research on Propaganda and Dictatorship," in Propaganda and Dictatorship, edited by Harwood L. Childs, Princeton, Princeton University Press, 1936, pp. 105-21.

Lazarsfeld, Paul F., "Audience Research in the Movie Field," Annals of the American Academy of Political and Social Science, November 1947, pp. 160-69.

Lebedev, Nikolai, Lenin, Stalin, partiya o kino (Lenin, Stalin and the Party on the Movie), Moscow, Gosudarstvennoye izdatel'stvo "Iskusstvo," 1938.

_____, Ocherk istorii kino SSSR (Outline of the History of the Movie in the U.S.S.R.), Moscow, Goskinoizdat, Volume I, 1947.

Lebedinsky, A., "Cinema Dramaturgy," Intercine, July 1935, pp. 401-04.

Lehmann-Haupt, Helmut, Art Under a Dictatorship, Oxford University Press, 1940.

Lejeune, Catherine A., Cinema, London, A. Maclehose, 1931.

Leonidov, O., "Novye kadry sovetskoi kinodramaturgii" (New Soviet Film-Writers), in Molodezh' sovetskogo kino (Youth of the Soviet Movies), edited by Semyon L. Ginsburg, Moscow, Goskinoizdat, 1938, pp. 66-73.

Leyda, Jay, "Advanced Training for Film Workers—Russia," Hollywood Quarterly, Volume I, Number 3, April 1946, pp. 232-84.

_____, "Prologue to the Russian Film," Hollywood Quarterly, Volume II, Number 1, October 1946, pp. 35-43, and Number 2, January 1947, pp. 164-73.

_____, "Two-Thirds of a Trilogy," Film Quarterly, Volume XII, Number 3, Spring 1959, pp. 18-22.

"Life Calls on a Russian Movie Star," Life, Volume 11, December 1, 1941, pp. 118-19.

London, Kurt, Seven Soviet Arts, New Haven, Yale University Press, 1938.

Lozowick, L., "Soviet Cinema: Eisenstein and Pudovkin," Theatre Arts, Volume 13, September 1929, pp. 664-75.

Macdonald, Dwight, "The Soviet Cinema, 1930-1938," Partisan Review, July 1938, pp. 37-50, and in August/September 1938, pp. 35-62.

_____, "Soviet Society and Its Cinema," Partisan Review, Winter 1939, pp. 80-95.

Manvell, Roger, Film, Harmondsworth Middlesex, Penguin Books, 1950.

_____, A Seat at the Cinema, London, Evan Brothers, 1951.

Marshall, Herbert P. J., "The Kino Olympiad: Moscow," Close Up, September 1930, pp. 168-76.

_____, "The Way of an Enthusiast," Close Up, November 1930, pp. 332-33.

_____, "Film Training and Production in the U.S.S.R.," Cine-Technician, April/May 1937, pp. 31-33.

_____, "Cinema in Russia," London Mercury and Bookman, Volume 38, October 1938, pp. 545-52.

_____, Soviet Cinema, London, Russia Today Society, 1945.

Marvell, R., "Day in Soviet Russia," New Statesman & Nation, Volume 22, August 30, 1941, p. 206.

Matthews, Tanya, Russian Child and Russian Wife, London, Victor Gollancz Ltd., 1949. Published in USA as Journey Between Freedoms, Philadelphia, Westminster Press, 1951.

Maxwell, Bertram W., The Soviet State: A Study of Bolshevik Rule, Topeka, Kansas, Steves and Wayburn, 1934.

_____, "Political Propaganda in Soviet Russia," in Propaganda and Dictatorship, edited by Harwood L. Childs, Princeton, Princeton University Press, 1936, pp. 61-79.

Mayer, J. P., Sociology of Film, London, Faber and Faber, 1946.

Messel, Rudolph, "The Film in Russia," in Twelve Studies in Soviet Russia, edited by Margaret I. Cole, London, Victor Gollancz, 1933.

Meyerowitz, H. V., "U.S.S.R. Goes Hollywood," World Film News, July 1936, pp. 11-14.

Middleton, Drew, "The Party Line Guides Russia's Movies," New York Times, July 27, 1947, Section VI, pp. 6-7.

Mikhailov, V., "Obkhodya glavnuyu temu" (Evading the Main Theme), Sovetskaya kultura, September 2, 1954, p. 2.

Miller, Warren, "Nakhimov and Pudovkin," Masses and Mainstream, February 1949, pp. 87-90.

Mirsky, Dmitri S., "Books and Films in Russia," Yale Review, March 1931, pp. 472-87.

_____, "Background of the Russian Films," London Mercury and Bookman, Volume 24, May 1931, pp. 53-64.

_____, "Soviet Films," Virginia Quarterly Review, Volume 7, October 1931, pp. 522-32.

Monosson, L. I., "The Soviet Cinematography," Society of Motion Picture Engineers' Journal, October 1930, pp. 509-27.

Montagu, Ivor, "Chapayev," New Statesman and Nation, Volume 9, February 2, 1935, pp. 139-40.

_____, "Soviet Cinema," in Britain on the Soviets: The Congress of Peace and Friendship with the USSR, London, Martin Lawrence, 1936, pp. 173-86.

"More Good Films for the Country," Izvestiya, September 4, 1951, p. 1. Translated in Current Digest of the Soviet Press, Volume III, Number 36, p. 9.

"Moscow Skies," New Statesman and Nation, Volume 29, March 17, 1945, p. 171.

"Motion Picture Propaganda in Russia," Bellman, Volume 25, August 3, 1918, p. 120.

Moussinac, Leon, "The Position of the Soviet Cinema," Experimental Cinema, 1931, Number 3, pp. 35-6.

"Movie Making Across the World," Theatre Arts, Volume 31, November 1947, pp. 60-65.

"New Russian Films," Living Age, Volume 332, May 15, 1927, pp. 929-30.

"New Trends in Films," International Literature, March 1935, p. 113.

Nicoll, Allardyce, Film and Theatre, New York, T. Crowell, 1936.

"October," Nation, Volume 127, December 26, 1928, pp. 720-21.

"Partisans in Action: 'People's Avengers,'" Newsweek, Volume 22, August 30, 1943, p. 80.

Pereslavtsev, V., "On Young Professional Cadres of the Soviet Cinema," Literaturnaya gazeta, November 24, 1951, pp. 2-4. Translated in Current Digest of the Soviet Press, Volume III, Number 47, pp. 3-5.

Piscator, Erwin, "A Theatre Director in the Soviet Cinema," New Theatre, January 1935, p. 14.

Pletnev, V., "The Soviet Film Industry," in Soviet Cinema, edited by A. Arosev, Moscow, VOKS, 1935, pp. 203-04.

"Polikushka," Labour Monthly, Volume 5, November 1923, pp. 293-96.

Popkin, Zelda, "Russia Goes to the Movies," Outlook, and Independent, Vol. 155, May 28, 1930, pp. 129-31.

_____, "Camera Explorers of the New Russia," Travel, Volume 58, December 1931, pp. 37-40.

Potamkin, Harry Alan, "Eisenstein and the Theory of Cinema," Hound and Horn, Volume IV, July/September 1933, pp. 678-89.

_____, The Eyes of the Movie, New York, International Publishers, 1934.

_____, "Film Problems of Soviet Russia," Experimental Cinema, February 1930, pp. 3-4, and June 1930, pp. 16-17.

_____, "Hollywood or Lenin Hills," New Theatre, April 1934, pp. 9-10.

_____, "The New Kino," Close Up, March 1931, pp. 64-69.

_____, "Pudovkin and the Revolutionary Cinema," Hound and Horn, Volume IV, April/June 1933, pp. 480-93.

_____, "Tendencies in the Soviet Film," New Masses, Volume VII, Number 12, p. 18.

Powell, Dilys, Films Since 1939, London, The British Council, Longmans Green, 1947.

Ptushko, A., "The Coming of a New Gulliver," Sight and Sound, London, British Film Institute, Volume IV, Number 14, Summer 1935, pp. 60-62.

Pudovkin, Vsevolod, "The Cinema," in The Soviet Comes of Age, edited by Sidney and Beatrice Webb, London, William Hodge, 1938.

_____, Soviet Historical Films, Moscow, VOKS, 1948.

_____, The Global Film," Hollywood Quarterly, Volume II, Number 4, July 1947, pp. 327-32.

_____, and K. Simonov, "About Young Cadres of Screen Directors and Scenario Writers," Literaturnaya gazeta, September 25, 1951, pp. 2-4. Translated in Current Digest of the Soviet Press, Volume III, Number 39, pp. 8-10.

"Raise Level of Soviet Film Art," Pravda, September 4, 1951, p. 1. Translated in Current Digest of the Soviet Press, Volume III, Number 36, p. 10.

Randall, R. G., "Russian Film," Nation, London, Volume 45, August 10, 1929, pp. 623-24.

Riley, John W., Jr., and Wilbur Schramm, The Reds Take a City: The Communist Occupation of Seoul, New Brunswick, Rutgers University Press, 1951.

Rokotov, Timofei, "A Failure and Its Reasons," International Literature, Moscow, State Literary-Art Publishing House, August 1937, pp. 97-99.

_____, "Recent Historical Films," International Literature, Moscow, State Literary-Art Publishing House, April 1938, pp. 98-104.

_____, "Soviet Cinema: On the Eve of the 20th Anniversary," International Literature, Moscow, State Literary-Art Publishing House, October/November 1937, pp. 193-201.

Roshal, Grigori, "The Soviet Film," Experiment in the Film, edited by Rober Manvell, London, Grey Walls Press, 1949, pp. 153-70.

Rosten, Leo, "Movies and Propaganda," Annals of the American Academy of Political and Social Science, November 1947, pp. 116-24.

Rotha, Paul, Celluloid: The Film Today, London, Longmans, Green, 1931.

_____, and Richard Griffith, The Film Till Now, New York, Funk and Wagnalls, 1949.

Rubin, Rose N., "Reorganization of the Film Industry," Bulletin on the Soviet Union, Washington, Embassy of the USSR, April 30, 1938, pp. 1, 4.

Sabant, Philippe, "Nouveaux Objectifs du Cinéma Sovietique," Cahiers du Cinema, Paris, Number 49, July 1955, pp. 53-58.

Salisbury, Harrison E., "What They Read and See in Moscow," New York Times, February 18, 1951, Section VI, pp. 21-29.

Schoeni, Helen, "Production Methods in Soviet Russia," Cinema Quarterly, Summer 1934, pp. 210-14.

Schrire, David, "Reply to 'U.S.S.R. Goes Hollywood,'" World Film News, August 1936, p. 25.

Schwab, Mack W., "Tiflis in the Caucasus Makes 30 Films a Year," World Film News, November 1936, p. 13.

Secretariat, Union of Soviet Writers, "About Young Cadres of Scenario Writers," Literaturnaya gazeta, December 13, 1951, p. 2. Translated in Current Digest of the Soviet Press, Volume III, Number 40, p. 7.

Seldes, Gilbert, "Some Russian Films," New Republic, Volume 59, July 3, 1929, pp. 179-80, and August 7, 1929, p. 317.

_____, The Great Audience, New York, Viking Press, 1950.

Semonov, Nikolai, "Toward New Successes of Soviet Film Art," Izvestiya, September 4, 1951, p. 3. Translated in Current Digest of the Soviet Press, Volume III, Number 36, pp. 9-10.

Seton, Marie, "The Making of the Russian 'Star,'" Close Up, June 1933, pp. 163-66.

_____, "Teaching Film in Russia," Film Art, Volume II, Number 5, Winter 1934, p. 24.

_____, "Contemporary Problems of the Soviet Cinema," Film Art, Spring 1934, p. 15.

_____, "New Trends in Soviet Cinema," Cinema Quarterly, Edinborough, Volume 3, Number 3, Spring 1935, pp. 149-52, and Number 4, Summer 1935, pp. 210-13.

_____, Eisenstein: A Biography, A. A. Wyn, 1954.

_____, "Second Thoughts on Eisenstein," Soviet Studies, Oxford, Basil Blackwell, Volume VI, Number 2, October 1954, pp. 113-23.

Shalyunovski, V., "'Gruziya-fil'm' v dolgu pered zritelyami" (Gruziya-Film in Debt to the Spectators), Sovetskaya kultura, September 18, 1954, p. 3.

Shelenkov, A., "Make Films More Quickly and Better," Sovetskaya kultura, April 26, 1955, p. 3. Translated and condensed in Current Digest of the Soviet Press, Volume VII, Number 21, pp. 8-9.

Shumyatsky, Boris, "Fifteen Years of Soviet Cinema," in Soviet Cinema, edited by A. Arosev, Moscow, VOKS, 1935, pp. 25-28.

"Siege of Stalingrad," New Statesman and Nation, Volume 25, April 17, 1943, p. 256.

Simpson, Celia, "Films in Moscow," Spectator, Volume 141, July 28, 1928, pp. 123-24.

Skouras, Charles P., "The Exhibitor," Annals of the American Academy of Political and Social Science, November 1947, pp. 26-30.

Slesinger, Donald, "The Film and Public Opinion," in Print, Radio and Film in a Democracy, edited by Douglas Waples, Chicago, University of Chicago Press, 1942, pp. 79-98.

Sokolov, I. V., Istoriya sovetskogo kinoiskusstva zvukovogo perioda (History of Soviet Film Art of the Sound Period), Moscow, Goskinoizdat, Volume I, 1946.

Solski, Waslaw, "The End of Sergei Eisenstein," Commentary, New York, Volume VII, March 1949, pp. 252-57.

"Sound Films in Soviet Republic," International Review of Educational Cinematography, January 1930, p. 75.

Soviet Cinema, edited by A. Arosev, Moscow, VOKS, 1935.

Soviet Cinematography, The, Bombay, People's Publishing House, 1950.

"Soviet Film Activities," International Review of Educational Cinematography, June 1930, pp. 757-60.

Soviet Films 1938-1939, edited by M. Borodin, L. Chernyarsky, and S. Yurovsky, Moscow, State Publishing House for Cinema Literature, 1939.

"Soviet Motion Picture Industry, The," Economic Review of the Soviet Union, January 1, 1930, pp. 8-10.

"Soviet Movies," Life, Volume 21, October 14, 1946, pp. 91-92.

"Statistics: The Cinematograph in the Soviet Republic," International Review of Educational Cinematography, January 1930, pp. 97-98.

Stern, Seymour, "Marie Seton: Eisenstein," Films in Review, Volume III, pp. 473-76, 534-39.

Stetsky, A., "To the Pinnacle of Art," Soviet Cinema, edited by A. Arosev, Moscow, VOKS, 1935, pp. 37-40.

Stevens, Edmund, This is Russia Un-censored, New York, Eton Books, 1951.

Swingler, R., "Sense of History in Soviet Films," Labour Monthly, Volume 24, February 1942, pp. 62-63.

"Ten Days that Shook the World," New Republic, Volume 57, November 21, 1928, pp. 17-18.

Towster, Julian, Political Power in the U.S.S.R., 1917-1947, New York, Oxford University Press, 1948.

Trauberg, Ilya, Young Soviet Masters of Cinema Art, Information Buro, VOKS, 1939.

Tretyakov, Sergei Mikhailovich, Der Film, Moscow, VOKS, 1928.

Troy, W., "Propaganda and Beauty," Nation, Volume 136, March 1, 1933, p. 242.

Turin, Victor, "The Problem of the New Film Language," Experimental Cinema, February 1931, pp. 11-12.

"Twenty-six Commissars," Nation, Volume 137, July 26, 1933, pp. 111-12.

Verlinsky, V. I., "The Motion Picture Industry in the Soviet Union," Society of Motion Picture Engineers' Journal, January 1935, p. 12.

Vertov, Dziga, "Kino Eye," Filmfront, Volume 1, Number 2, January 7, 1935, pp. 6-8.

von Eckardt, Hans, Russia, New York, Knopf, 1932.

Watts, Richard, Jr., "Soviet Cinema Art," Research Bulletin on the Soviet Union, May 16, 1936, pp. 1-5.

Weinberg, Herman, "Russia," Close Up, June 1933, pp. 175-81.

_____, "Vsevolod Pudovkin," Films in Review, Volume IV, Number 7, August/September 1953, pp. 325-27.

Williams, Albert Rhys, The Soviets, New York, Harcourt, Brace, 1937.

Wilson, Edmund, "Eisenstein in Hollywood," New Republic, Volume 68, November 4, 1931, pp. 320-22.

Wollenberg, H. H., "Round the World's Studios," Film Review, London, Penguin Books, Number 3, August 1947, pp. 36-38, and Number 4, October 1947, p. 25.

"Writers and the Screen," Literaturnaya gazeta, September 1, 1951, p. 3. Translated in Current Digest of the Soviet Press, Volume III, Number 36, p. 11.

Yeremin, D., 30 let sovetskoi kinematografii: Sbornik statei (30 Years of Soviet Cineamtography: A Collection of Articles), Moscow, Goskinoizdat, 1950.

Yesuitov, N., "Basic Trends in Soviet Film Art," Soviet Cinema, edited by A. Arosev, Moscow, VOKS, 1935, pp. 51-67.

_____, "Cinema," Art in the U.S.S.R., edited by Geoffrey Holme, New York, Studio Publications, 1935, pp. 95-96, 113-22.

Yurenev, R., "More and Better Scenarios," Pravda, August 7, 1955, p. 2. Condensed and translated in Current Digest of the Soviet Press, Volume VII, Number 32, p. 29.

APPENDIX

The three variables used to measure the extent of political progaganda content--time period, political affiliation of the hero, and problem-- should not be considered independent variables, even though they measure different dimensions of content. Rather, the three measures of propaganda content ought to be considered part of a composite index.

An internal analysis of the composite index for political propaganda content reveals some interesting changes over time. For films released during the period 1941-1945, for example, the most common type of rating is "1" (non-Komsomol, non-Party) on <u>political affiliation</u>, "6" (contemporary) on <u>time period</u> depicted in the film, and "5" (social problem, Communist solution) on <u>problem and resolution</u>. More than one-third of all the films produced during the years 1941-1945 are rated "1," "6" and "5"—abbreviated "165" on the chart below.

Rating	Time Period				
	1923-1928	1929-1933	1934-1940	1941-1945	1946-1952
165	7%	18%	23%	38%	29%
465	1	1	0	1	10
665	0	0	1	2	13
114	3	1	7	12	0
145	2	2	10	1	0
Others	87	78	59	46	48
Total	100%	100%	100%	100%	100%
Number of Films	(135)	(88)	(150)	(88)	(62)

Note, however, that the rating "165" is not as common for films released at other times, particularly in the earlier years of the Soviet regime. During these earlier years, in fact, there was such great variety in film content that no other single rating predominates. During the later years, however, a few other scores (e.g., "465") were used to rate as much as ten percent (or more) of the entire output in these particular periods.

Two ratings stand out among the scores for films released in the post-war period. The rating "465"—"4" (local Communist Party official) on political affiliation, "6" (contemporary) on time period depicted in the film, and "5" (social problem, Communist resolution) on problem and reso-lution—accounts for ten percent of all the rated film content during the post-war period, 1946-1952. The rating "665"—"6" (chieftain of the Communist Party) on political affiliation, "6" (contemporary) on time period, and "5" (social problem, Communist resolution) on problem and resolution—accounts for even more than ten percent of the films released during the years 1946-1952.

During the war years, 1941-1945, the rating "114" stands out—"1" (non-Komsomol, non-Party) on political affiliation, "1" (more than 100 years ago) on time period and "4" (social problem, "progressive" solution) on problem and resolution. This rating generally describes films about Russian (or Ukrainian) historical figures who were depicted in heroic pro-portion to arouse nationalistic and patriotic sentiments in the population at a time when the nation was again under attack by an ancient foe.

During the years 1934-1940, too, there were some films rated "114," about patriotic historical figures, but even more films of the type rated "145" were released. These are generally films about the 1905 Russian Revolution, the 1917 Communist Revolution, or the Civil War of 1918-1921, with non-Komsomol, non-Party heroes confronting social problems that are ultimately resolved in approved Bolshevik fashion.

A more detailed table of ratings appears on the following page.

	Time Period									
Rating	1923–1928		1929–1933		1934–1940		1941–1945		1946–1952	
	#	%	#	%	#	%	#	%	#	%
005	-	0	2	2	1	1	1	1	1	2
030	-	0	2	2	-	0	-	0	-	0
040	-	0	2	2	-	0	-	0	-	0
045	3	2	4	5	1	1	-	0	1	2
050	4	3	2	2	-	0	-	0	-	0
055	3	2	1	1	-	0	-	0	2	3
060	6	4	6	7	-	0	1	1	3	5
065	3	2	6	7	4	3	4	5	-	0
100	5	4	1	1	-	0	1	1	-	0
111	5	4	-	0	2	1	5	6	1	2
112	1	1	1	1	1	1	-	0	-	0
114	4	3	1	1	11	7	10	12	-	0
120	-	0	1	1	2	1	4	5	-	0
121	5	4	-	0	4	3	1	1	-	0
122	4	3	1	1	6	4	4	5	-	0
123	1	1	1	1	-	0	-	0	-	0
124	6	4	-	0	5	3	1	1	4	6
132	4	3	-	0	1	1	-	0	-	0
135	-	0	-	0	2	1	-	0	2	3
140	5	4	1	1	-	0	-	0	-	0
142	6	4	1	1	-	0	-	0	-	0
143	2	1	1	1	-	0	-	0	-	0
144	4	3	1	1	1	1	-	0	-	0
145	3	2	2	2	15	10	1	1	-	0
150	-	0	2	2	-	0	-	0	-	0
155	4	3	3	4	2	1	-	0	2	3
160	1	1	3	4	5	3	3	3	-	0
161	5	4	-	0	6	4	3	3	3	5
162	3	2	1	1	2	1	-	0	-	0
163	-	0	2	2	-	0	-	0	-	0
164	4	3	2	2	1	1	-	0	2	3
165	9	7	15	18	36	23	33	38	18	29
255	3	2	-	0	1	1	-	0	-	0
261	-	0	-	0	3	2	-	0	-	0
265	8	6	4	5	11	7	3	3	-	0
355	4	3	1	1	1	1	-	0	-	0
365	4	3	4	5	7	4	2	2	2	3
465	1	1	1	1	-	0	1	1	6	10
545	-	0	-	0	3	2	1	1	-	0
635	-	0	-	0	1	1	-	0	2	3
645	-	0	-	0	4	3	1	1	2	3
665	-	0	-	0	1	1	2	2	8	13
Others	15	11	13	15	10	7	6	7	3	5
Total	135	100	88	100	150	100	38	100	62	100

The Arno Press Cinema Program

THE LITERATURE OF CINEMA

Series I & II

Agate, James. **Around Cinemas**. 1946.

Agate, James. **Around Cinemas**. (Second Series). 1948.

American Academy of Political and Social Science. **The Motion Picture in Its Economic and Social Aspects**, edited by Clyde L. King. **The Motion Picture Industry**, edited by Gordon S. Watkins. *The Annals*, November, 1926/1927.

L'Art Cinematographique, Nos. 1-8. 1926-1931.

Balcon, Michael, Ernest Lindgren, Forsyth Hardy and Roger Manvell. **Twenty Years of British Film, 1925-1945.** 1947.

Bardèche, Maurice and Robert Brasillach. **The History of Motion Pictures,** edited by Iris Barry. 1938.

Benoit-Levy, Jean. **The Art of the Motion Picture.** 1946.

Blumer, Herbert. **Movies and Conduct.** 1933.

Blumer, Herbert and Philip M. Hauser. **Movies, Delinquency, and Crime.** 1933.

Buckle, Gerard Fort. **The Mind and the Film.** 1926.

Carter, Huntly. **The New Spirit in the Cinema.** 1930.

Carter, Huntly. **The New Spirit in the Russian Theatre, 1917-1928.** 1929.

Carter, Huntly. **The New Theatre and Cinema of Soviet Russia.** 1924.

Charters, W. W. **Motion Pictures and Youth.** 1933.

Cinema Commission of Inquiry. **The Cinema: Its Present Position and Future Possibilities.** 1917.

Dale, Edgar. **Children's Attendance at Motion Pictures.** Dysinger, Wendell S. and Christian A. Ruckmick. **The Emotional Responses of Children to the Motion Picture Situation.** 1935.

Dale, Edgar. **The Content of Motion Pictures.** 1935.

Dale, Edgar. **How to Appreciate Motion Pictures.** 1937.

Dale, Edgar, Fannie W. Dunn, Charles F. Hoban, Jr., and Etta Schneider. **Motion Pictures in Education: A Summary of the Literature.** 1938.

Davy, Charles. **Footnotes to the Film.** 1938.

Dickinson, Thorold and Catherine De la Roche. **Soviet Cinema.** 1948.

Dickson, W. K. L., and Antonia Dickson. **History of the Kinetograph, Kinetoscope and Kinetophonograph.** 1895.

Forman, Henry James. **Our Movie Made Children.** 1935.

Freeburg, Victor Oscar. **The Art of Photoplay Making.** 1918.

Freeburg, Victor Oscar. **Pictorial Beauty on the Screen.** 1923.

Hall, Hal, editor. **Cinematographic Annual,** 2 vols. 1930/1931.

Hampton, Benjamin B. **A History of the Movies.** 1931.

Hardy, Forsyth. **Scandinavian Film.** 1952.

Hepworth, Cecil M. **Animated Photography: The A B C of the Cinematograph.** 1900.

Hoban, Charles F., Jr., and Edward B. Van Ormer. **Instructional Film Research 1918-1950.** 1950.

Holaday, Perry W. and George D. Stoddard. **Getting Ideas from the Movies.** 1933.

Hopwood, Henry V. **Living Pictures.** 1899.

Hulfish, David S. **Motion-Picture Work.** 1915.

Hunter, William. **Scrutiny of Cinema.** 1932.

Huntley, John. **British Film Music.** 1948.

Irwin, Will. **The House That Shadows Built.** 1928.

Jarratt, Vernon. **The Italian Cinema.** 1951.

Jenkins, C. Francis. **Animated Pictures.** 1898.

Lang, Edith and George West. **Musical Accompaniment of Moving Pictures.** 1920.

London, Kurt. **Film Music.** 1936.

Lutz, E [dwin] G [eorge]. **The Motion-Picture Cameraman.** 1927.

Manvell, Roger. **Experiment in the Film.** 1949.

Marey, Etienne Jules. **Movement.** 1895.

Martin, Olga J. **Hollywood's Movie Commandments.** 1937.

Mayer, J. P. **Sociology of Film: Studies and Documents.** 1946. New Introduction by J. P. Mayer.

Münsterberg, Hugo. **The Photoplay: A Psychological Study.** 1916.
Nicoll, Allardyce. **Film and Theatre.** 1936.

Noble, Peter. **The Negro in Films.** 1949.

Peters, Charles C. **Motion Pictures and Standards of Morality.** 1933.

Peterson, Ruth C. and L. L. Thurstone. **Motion Pictures and the Social Attitudes of Children.** Shuttleworth, Frank K. and Mark A. May. **The Social Conduct and Attitudes of Movie Fans.** 1933.

Phillips, Henry Albert. **The Photodrama.** 1914.

Photoplay Research Society. **Opportunities in the Motion Picture Industry.** 1922.

Rapée, Erno. **Encyclopaedia of Music for Pictures.** 1925.

Rapée, Erno. **Motion Picture Moods for Pianists and Organists.** 1924.

Renshaw, Samuel, Vernon L. Miller and Dorothy P. Marquis. **Children's Sleep.** 1933.

Rosten, Leo C. **Hollywood: The Movie Colony, The Movie Makers.** 1941.

Sadoul, Georges. **French Film.** 1953.

Screen Monographs I, 1923-1937. 1970.

Screen Monographs II, 1915-1930. 1970.

Sinclair, Upton. **Upton Sinclair Presents William Fox.** 1933.

Talbot, Frederick A. **Moving Pictures.** 1912.

Thorp, Margaret Farrand. **America at the Movies.** 1939.

Wollenberg, H. H. **Fifty Years of German Film.** 1948.

RELATED BOOKS AND PERIODICALS

Allister, Ray. **Friese-Greene: Close-Up of an Inventor.** 1948.

Art in Cinema: A Symposium of the Avant-Garde Film, edited by Frank Stauffacher. 1947.

The Art of Cinema: Selected Essays. New Foreword by George Amberg. 1971.

Balázs, Béla. **Theory of the Film.** 1952.

Barry, Iris. **Let's Go to the Movies.** 1926.

de Beauvoir, Simone. **Brigitte Bardot and the Lolita Syndrome.** 1960.

Carrick, Edward. **Art and Design in the British Film.** 1948.

Close Up. Vols. 1-10, 1927-1933 (all published).

Cogley, John. **Report on Blacklisting. Part I: The Movies.** 1956.

Eisenstein, S. M. **Que Viva Mexico!** 1951.

Experimental Cinema. 1930-1934 (all published).

Feldman, Joseph and Harry. **Dynamics of the Film.** 1952.

Film Daily Yearbook of Motion Pictures. Microfilm, 18 reels, 35 mm. 1918-1969.

Film Daily Yearbook of Motion Pictures. 1970.

Film Daily Yearbook of Motion Pictures. (Wid's Year Book). 3 vols., 1918-1922.

The Film Index: A Bibliography. Vol. I: The Film as Art. 1941.

Film Society Programmes. 1925-1939 (all published).

Films: A Quarterly of Discussion and Analysis. Nos. 1-4, 1939-1940 (all published).

Flaherty, Frances Hubbard. **The Odyssey of a Film-Maker: Robert Flaherty's Story.** 1960.

General Bibliography of Motion Pictures, edited by Carl Vincent, Riccardo Redi, and Franco Venturini. 1953.

Hendricks, Gordon. **Origins of the American Film.** 1961-1966. New Introduction by Gordon Hendricks.

Hound and Horn: Essays on Cinema, 1928-1934. 1971.

Huff, Theodore. Charlie Chaplin. 1951.

Kahn, Gordon. Hollywood on Trial. 1948.

New York Times Film Reviews, 1913-1968. 1970.

Noble, Peter. Hollywood Scapegoat: The Biography of Erich von Stroheim. 1950.

Robson, E. W. and M. M. The Film Answers Back. 1939.

Seldes, Gilbert. An Hour with the Movies and the Talkies. 1929.

Weinberg, Herman G., editor. Greed. 1971.

Wollenberg, H. H. Anatomy of the Film. 1947.

Wright, Basil. The Use of the Film. 1948.

DISSERTATIONS ON FILM

Karpf, Stephen L. The Gangster Film: Emergence, Variation and Decay of a Genre, 1930-1940. First publication, 1973.

Lounsbury, Myron O. The Origins of American Film Criticism, 1909-1939. First publication, 1973.

Sands, Pierre N. A Historical Study of the Academy of the Motion Picture Arts and Sciences (1927-1947). First publication, 1973.

North, Joseph H. The Early Development of the Motion Picture, 1887-1909. First publication, 1973.

Rimberg, John. The Motion Picture in the Soviet Union, 1918-1952. First publication, 1973.

Wolfe, Glenn J. Vachel Lindsay: The Poet as Film Theorist. First publication, 1973.